Thomas Phaer and The Boke of Chyldren (1544)

Thomas Phaer
and
The Boke of Chyldren (1544)

MEDIEVAL & RENAISSANCE

TEXTS & STUDIES

Volume 201

Thomas Phaer
and
The Boke of Chyldren (1544)

by

RICK BOWERS

Arizona Center for Medieval and Renaissance Studies
Tempe, Arizona
1999

To my wife Katherine

CONTENTS

Preface	ix
Abbreviations	xi
Photograph of Copy Text	xii
Introduction	
The Author	1
The Text	10
The Preface to *The Boke of Chyldren*	27
The Boke of Chyldren	31
Textual Notes	79
Glossary of Authors	83
Glossary of Medicinal Herbs and Plants	87
Works Cited	97

PREFACE

Thomas Phaer's *The Boke of Chyldren* (1544) is the first English book on pediatrics. The text, written in English for an English readership, popularizes and communicates medicine in a radically new way. by stressing the importance of the vernacular, and by considering children as material, medical subjects requiring specialized health care. Contemporary focus stressed catechismal training or ignored children altogether as negligible, unformed adults. Extremely high infant mortality combined with death from early childhood diseases and general epidemic threat to ensure children an emotionally-distanced place in early modern English society. Poised between folk beliefs and a rudimentary empiricism, Phaer's book, which enjoyed multiple reprintings throughout the last half of the sixteenth century, attempts to close that distance.

Anyone coming in contact with this little medical tract stresses its importance and singularity. In 1925, John Ruhräh declared Phaer "the Father of English Pediatrics," adding, "the first book on pediatrics printed in English should not be permitted to remain a curiosity, known only to medical bibliophiles and doubtless not even to many of them" (147). Yet the only modern edition of *The Boke of Chyldren* (Neale and Wallis 1955) presents the book as just such a curiosity by merely reproducing the 1553 imprint, unaware of the first edition of 1544 buried in Jehan Goeurot's *The Regiment of Life* and ignoring all other editions of the period A facsimile text issued in 1976 in the English Experience series (No 802) merely reprints the second edition of Goeurot's book with no introduction or textual apparatus whatsoever.

The Boke of Children first appears in *The Regiment of Life* (*STC* 11967; London, 1544), the only extant copy of which is located at the Huntington Library, San Marino, California. *STC* vol. 2 notes another copy in the Library of the Royal College of Physicians of London, but the attribution is in error. (See Textual Notes, 79.)

My annotated text of *The Boke of Chyldren*, based on the unique copy in the Huntington Library, is lightly modernized in order to facilitate reading. Throughout, I have regularized all *i/j* and *u/v* reversals as well as the use of long *s*. I have also consistently regularized use of "then/than," "see/se," and "too/to." Proper nouns have been consistently capitalized. Archaic contractions have been expanded and ampersands spelled out. Although I have modernized punctuation, I have avoided wholesale modernization in order to retain the archaic charm of Phaer's prose. All exemplars have been collated with notes concerning basic meanings and textual notes on editorial choices gathered at the conclusion. Separate glossaries of historical names and medicinal herbs provide easy reference.

A critical introduction presents the fullest biographical account of Thomas Phaer (parts of which appeared previously in *Notes and Queries* 239 and *Renaissance and Reformation* 21) in addition to critical grounding in medical history and cultural communication. *The Boke of Chyldren* deserves reconsideration both as an early example of English prose style and as historicized medical development. By lightly modernizing the text, I hope to stay true to Phaer's own populist mandate, as he himself puts it in his preface: "to shewe the remedyes that God hath created for the use of man to distrybute in Englysshe to them that are unlerned" (27).

This project, for the learned and "unlerned," took initial shape during the term of a study leave at the University of Alberta 1993/94.

ABBREVIATIONS

CJ	*Journals of the House of Commons*
CPR	*Calendar of Patent Rolls*
OED	*The Oxford English Dictionary*
STC	*Short Title Catalogue of English Books 1475–1640* (2nd ed.)

The boke of chyldren.

O begyn a treatyſe of the cure of chyldren, it ſhoulde ſeme expedyent, that we ſhuld declare ſomewhat of the principles as of the generacion, the beinge in the wombe, the tyme of procedyng, the maner of the byrth, the byndyng of the nauyll, ſettynge of the membres, lauatories, vnctions, ſwathinges, & entreatementes, with the circumſtaunces of theſe and many other, which if J ſhuld reherce in particles, it wolde requyre both a longer tyme, and encreaſe into a greater volume. But foraſmoch, as the mooſt of theſe thynges are verye tryte & manifeſt: ſome pertaynyng onely to ye office of any dwyfe, other for the reue-

b   rence

The Boke of Chyldren (1544)

INTRODUCTION

The Author

A hundred years after his death in August 1560, Thomas Phaer was still remembered as "a person of a mutable mind" (Wood 315). Scientist, classicist, physician, legal theorist, member of Parliament, and general man of letters, Phaer certainly followed a varied and nontraditional career pattern. Put simply, he was a Renaissance polymath. And all his endeavors in medicine, art, law, and classical learning were linked by a reliance—even an insistence—on English as his preferred mode of scholarly communication.

His publications are socially conscious and purposely English, including an early translation of *The Aeneid* (that key text of British etiology), English legal texts, a popular translation of the French medical text entitled *The Regiment of Life*, and most especially his own—and England's first—pediatrics text, *The Boke of Chyldren* (1544), wherein Phaer rhetorically demands:

> Why grutche they [Latinist physicians] phisik to come forth in Englysshe? wolde they have no man to knowe but onely they? (27).

Clearly, Phaer's mission is to popularize pediatric care and inform his fellow citizens of health care issues specific to the treatment of children. English, not Latin, is the language proper to informing English parents. Phaer probably felt licensed in his critique of Latin by Sir Thomas Elyot's defense of vernacular English a few years earlier in *The Castel of Helth*. "But if phisitions be angry, that I have wryten phisike in englyshe, let theym remembre that the grekes wrate in greke, the Romanes in latyne, Avicena and the other in Arabike, whiche were their owne propre and maternal tonges" (A4v). Phaer rehearses a similar line of argument in his own preface to *The Boke of Chyldren*. Such cultural specificity played well in England in the first half of the sixteenth century, a period which had seen popular translation of Scripture into English by

Tyndale and Coverdale in 1525 and 1535 respectively, and had also experienced the rigorous social consolidation of the realm under Henry VIII as a religious and cultural entity detached from continental Europe.

Thomas Phaer presents himself as very much a middle-class Tudor man of a conservative temperament with distinctive scholarly abilities, strongly-conceived public responsibilities, and information to share. Yet little is known for sure about his early life. He seems to have been born in Norwich sometime in 1510 or thereabouts, and was educated at Oxford University and at Lincoln's Inn. His early residence in the household of William Paulet, 1st Marquess of Winchester, no doubt helped his career advancement in law and politics and may have secured for him his appointment as solicitor to the council of the Marches of Wales. Phaer says nearly as much in his dedication to Queen Mary of the first seven books of the "*Eneidos of Virgill*," printed in 1558. "I have been preferred to your service by your right noble and faithfull counsailour Willyam lorde Marqueis of Winchester, my firste brynger up and patrone" (A2r). Phaer seems to have first appeared in print some twenty years earlier with the publication of a legal text entitled *Natura Brevium, Newly Corrected in Englysshe* (1530?). His name, at least, has always been popularly associated with this otherwise anonymous volume, the *STC* according him the status of translator. This he followed with a comprehensive formula book of legal documents and precedents entitled *A Newe Boke of Presidentes* (1543), concluding his preface with a nod in the direction of the vernacular and with a distinct consciousness about the education of children·

> And therfore is it compounded both in English and in Latyne, to the intent it may be the easelyer taken and perceyved of them that are but meanely learned in the Latyne tonge, and also for suche as wyll applye theyr chyldren to the readynge and understandyng of common evydences and wrytynges. Wherin I beseche God that they maye procede both to theyr owne commodytie, and profyte of theyr poore neyghbours (A2v).

This accessible text was so popular that it went through twenty-seven editions to 1656 and was used by the great Elizabethan jurist Thomas Egerton when he was a student at Lincoln's Inn (Jones 63–64). Certainly Phaer's legal expertise prepared him for a career on the bench and in parliament even though Fuller contends that "the Study of the Law did not fadge well with him, which caused him to change his copy, and proceed Doctor in Physick" (12). In fact Phaer combined his professional intellectual pursuits within a social concern that would move him into medical publication and active political involvement.

Indeed the year 1544 saw his translation of Jehan Goeurot's medical compendium *The Regiment of Life* out of French and into the company of Phaer's own medical efforts: *A Goodly Bryefe Treatyse of the Pestylence*, *A Declaration of the Veynes*, and *The Boke of Chyldren* The octavo, containing all four titles, was printed in London by Edward Whytchurche, and exists today in a single copy at the Huntington Library in San Marino, California. Phaer's was clearly a populist mission of education and concern, picking up where Latin authorities had left off, as set forth in the preface to his treatise on pestilence:

> This disease when it ones beginneth enfecteth none so moche as the common people, among whom it is not gyven to al men to understande the forsayd volumes, yf they had them present, moch lesse can they get theyr health by theyr owne ymaginacions or experimentes, specially when almost no phisition wyll vouchesafe to visite any suche infected of the common sorte (so great is the daunger of this cruell syckenes) by reason wherof the pacientes cast themselves oftentymes into despeyre (L6v).

Combine this with Phaer's avowed purpose in *The Boke of Chyldren*, "to do them good that have moost nede" (27), and one begins to detect a real sense of medical compassion, public spirit, and social responsibility in this particular author.

Medical historian John Ruhräh calls Phaer the "Father of English Pediatrics" (147), and modern *Eneidos* editor Steven Lally refers to him as "a humanist and avant-garde scientific mind" (xiv). Phaer's humanism, however, was not the academic variety of intellectuals such as Erasmus, John Colet, or a whole new class of theoretical Protestant divines. Instead he was publicly engaged, was busy in the day-to-day practice of law and medicine and as public representative and government agent. Indeed Phaer eschews classical academic debate in itself to present an interventionist public stance, a stance of populist social concern especially for children. Can it be a complete coincidence that in 1547, during Phaer's first term as member of Parliament for Carmarthen Boroughs, a bill "for the nursing of Children in Wales" (*CJ* 1. 3, 4) should be introduced? Likewise, that William Turner, author of the first English-language herbal, and Thomas Phaer, author of the first English-language pediatrics text, both sat as Members of Parliament in the 1547 session of the House of Commons (Bindoff 3: 102, 490)?

Phaer served four terms under three monarchs as an MP from Wales, representing first Carmarthen Boroughs in 1547 before being returned from Cardigan Boroughs in 1555, 1558, and 1559 A fortunate marriage to widow Anne Revell no doubt aided him in taking a 21-year lease of demesne lands of the lordship of Cilgerran in November 1549. From this point on, Phaer made his permanent address in the forest of Cilgerran This would be his home constituency His leased property overlapped into Pembrokeshire, but Phaer was considered a Cardiganshire resident. His residence and prominence no doubt explain his nomination as sheriff for the region in 1552 Although another name was "pricked by the king as chosen" (*CPR* 1553, 387), Phaer went on to serve the region in a variety of official capacities. And yet he seems to have been less than sanguine about his constituency, to judge by the citation in Bindoff's *The House of Commons 1509-1558*.

> Cardiganshire was enlarged and consolidated at the Union. Thomas Phaer described it as "very bare .. and mountainous, all along the coast no trade of merchandise but all full of rocks and dangers." The few roads were unmetalled and travellers were vexed by bandits who the president of the council in the marches thought had the support of the local gentry (1 271).

Clearly this country doctor was in touch with his rural environment, even though such a relatively remote location would be unusual for a medical writer of the early Renaissance when most authoritative physicians lived either in London or in one of the university towns.

Throughout the 1550s Phaer served publicly as steward of Cilgerran and constable of the castle there, as crown searcher and customs officer in the port of Milford Haven, as solicitor to the council in the marches of Wales, and as Justice of the Peace for Cardiganshire. He would be well remunerated for these official duties, while a position in coastal customs would ensure an almost unlimited opportunity for graft. Yet Phaer seems to have been trusted throughout. On orders from the Marquess of Winchester, he prepared a report on harbors and customs administration in Wales, a report enrolled after his death on Queen Elizabeth's memoranda roll for Hilary term 1562 (Bindoff 3: 103) Although a loyal public servant under Queen Mary, Phaer enjoyed the trust of Elizabeth I's new administration as well, and his name is listed on the Pardon roll for the first year of Elizabeth's reign: "Thomas Phaer late of Kylgerran, co. Pembroke, *alias* M.D." (*CPR* 1558-60, 203). His inclusion is a formality—but an obligatory one for anybody seeking government commission or public trust.

This lawyer, physician, and public administrator also had literary projects underway, and it is perhaps through his early translation of *The Aeneid* that he is best known. Other translators such as Gavin Douglas, the Earl of Surrey, and Richard Stanyhurst had offered the poem in English, but Phaer's *Eneidos*, completed by Thomas Twyne and running to unprecedented multiple editions, can rightly be called "the *Aeneid* of the English Renaissance" (Lally xii). Certainly Phaer was the first Englishman to attempt a translation of the entire epic, although his death prevented him from seeing the project to its conclusion. Keeping close account of time he spent translating, Phaer began his *Eneidos* on May 9, 1555, and averaged about twenty days work per book, work which he considered to be, in his words, "my pastyme in all my vacations" (1558, A2r) He published *The seven first bookes of the Eneidos of Virgill* in 1558, followed by an edition of the first nine books after his death, brought out in 1562 by fellow MP William Wightman. It wasn't until 1584 that the entire *Eneidos* was completed by Twyne, but Phaer's nationalist perspective on the English language is in evidence from the very first, declaring his Virgil to be a "defence of my countrey language which I have heard discommended of many, and estemyd of some to bee more than barbarous" (*Eneidos* 1558, X2r)

If Phaer seems a bit truculent on the topic of his Englishness, bear in mind that his legal training no doubt groomed his balanced instinct for redress. In fact, his first published poem took the form of a defense, appearing as preface to Peter Betham's translation of Jacopo di Porcia's *The Preceptes of Warre* (1544). The text's printer, Edward Whytchurche, had brought out Phaer's *Newe Boke of Presidentes* the year before, and was probably preparing the *Regiment of Life* compendium for the press at the same time as he was printing Betham's work In any case, Phaer's rhyme royal stanza for *The Preceptes of Warre* was as vaguely donnish as suggestive for a man embarking on a life of politics and publication:

> Chyefest is peace, but yf by extremitye
> Thou be enforced to fyght for thyne owne,
> Learne here the science and actes of chyvaldrye,
> Pollicies, and privities, to many men unknowen:
> Wherby thyne enemyes may be overthrowen.
> In suche a necessitie shalt thou never fynde
> Suche an other treasure: kepe it wel in minde. (A7v)

A man who would thrive publicly under the Tudor administrations of mid-sixteenth-century England had better be politic, defensive, and clearheaded about the precepts of debate, civic struggle, and conflict.

At about the same time as Phaer was preparing his *Eneidos*, he also contributed a poetic piece on Owen Glendower to *The Mirror for Magistrates* compendium. Entitled "Howe Owen Glendour seduced by false prophesies took upon him to be prince of Wales," this cautionary moral poem contains thirty-four verses which are vaguely Spenserian in form. Phaer was associated in this effort with contributors George Ferrers and Sir Thomas Chaloner, fellow MPs. He also knew the *Mirror* compiler, William Baldwin, through Edward Whytchurche in whose printing house Baldwin had worked. The 1578 edition of the *Mirror* even contains William Baldwin's note of light editorial facetiousness at the conclusion of Phaer's poem: "Whan mayster Phaer had ended the Tragedy of thys hunger starven Prynce of Wales, it was well liked of all the company that a Saxon would speake so mutch for a Brytton, then sodenly one found" (Campbell 131). Phaer, however, although born a "Saxon," was now a Welsh resident and had represented his region publicly for years. He clearly had gained an adopted "Welshness" about himself, a cultural capacity that set him apart and perhaps aided his reputation for poetry.

And his poetic ability was clearly recognized, as noted by Anthony à Wood "he was much famed among the academians for his sufficiencies in the art of poetry" (316). Indeed, nearly thirty years after Phaer's death, no less an authority than George Puttenham, in *The Arte of English Poesie* (1589), looked back a generation in considering "*the most commended writers in our English Poesie*," and declared. "In Queenes Maries time florished above any other Doctour *Phaer* one that was well learned and excellently well translated into English verse Heroicall certaine bookes of *Virgils Æneidos*" (73, 75). Arthur Hall, too, some eight years earlier opened his translation of Homer with a dedication wherein he confesses to prolonged scholarly torpor and mental disquiet, claiming, however, with some feeling that it was Phaer who finally stimulated him.

> *But when I lighted on* M. Thomas Phaers Virgilian *Englishe, quoth I, what have I done? am I become senslesse, to travaile to be laughed at, to presume, and to be scorned, and to put forth my selfe and not to be received: for I was so abashed looking upon* M. Phaers Heroicall Virgill, *and my Satiricall* Homer, *as I cried out, envying* Virgils *prosperitie* (A3v).

Consider also the preface of Thomas Nashe to Robert Greene's romance narrative, *Menaphon* (1589). Nashe, with characteristic enthusiasm, inveighed against pretences to learning in general, itemizing by contrast distinguished literary figures, Phaer among them:

> Master *Phaer* likewise is not to be forgot in regard of his famous *Virgil*, whose heavenly verse had it not bin blemisht by his hautie thoghts *England* might have long insulted in his wit, and *corrigat qui potest* have been subscribed to his workes (6. 20).

Clearly, it was difficult to improve on Phaer in his own time, his reputation for "hautie thoghts" perhaps suggesting the extent of his wide-ranging authority and self-confidence. In any case, reprints of Phaer's publications carried on well into the next century.

Renowned as a physician, author and legislator, Thomas Phaer seems consciously to have settled accounts with himself late in life. On February 6, 1559, Phaer graduated MB from Oxford and proceeded MD the following month. Clearly a formality, his supplication for the Bachelor's degree included Phaer's statement that "he had practised medicine for twenty years, and had made experiments about poisons and antidotes" (Lee 1026). Writing on provincial medical history of the period, R. S. Roberts notes that university licences "to practice medicine throughout England" were usually granted at Oxford at the same time as the MB degree with the applicant nearly always already in practice This was clearly the case with Thomas Phaer As historian Nancy Siraisi puts it, "throughout the twelfth to fifteenth centuries (and for long thereafter), the task of acquiring medical expertise was pursued in a variety of contexts and at widely varying levels of formal organization, intellectualization, and sophistication. Medical education was formally acquired in the university classroom or informally through private study or shared experience" (50). Through practice, publication, and retroactive official imprimatur, Phaer seems to have involved himself in all the possibilities for gaining medical expertise.

And he seems to have lived the literary life right up to the end as well. Having concluded book five of *Eneidos* on May 4, 1556, Phaer mentions escaping an accident at Carmarthen which may or may not have involved his official duties there as customs searcher (Bindoff 3: 103). A serious injury to his right hand sometime after April 3, 1560, ended his translating at line 298 of the tenth book of *Eneidos*, and he died later that August. His will, dated August 12, names his wife as sole executrix and provides generously for his daughters Elynor, Mary, and Elizabeth He also directed that his wife apply £5 to an unspecified purpose "where she doth knowe, by an appointemente betwene her and me" (Cunningham 4) which may or may not mean auxiliary burial rites of the Roman Catholic church. Phaer also requested that his influential Protestant friend George Ferrers select a scriptural passage "graven in brasse" (Cunningham 3) for his gravestone.

Phaer's *Eneidos*, however, lived on. According to his literary executor, William Wightman, Phaer requested that the second edition of his *Eneidos* be dedicated to the powerful, rising Protestant politician Sir Nicholas Bacon, Elizabeth's Lord Keeper of the Great Seal. Consequently, in 1562 Wightman saw Phaer's nine-book *Eneidos* through the press: "*The Nyne Fyrst Bookes of the Eneidos of Virgil* converted into Englishe vearse by Thomas Phaer Doctour of Phisike, with so muche of the tenthe Booke as since his death coulde be founde in unperfit papers at his house in Kilgarran forest in Penbroke shyre." In the dedication, Wightman is as forceful as he is personal:

> Whilest God gave lyfe and health to Thomas Phaer Doctour of Phisike, I had some moore frendly familiaritie with him then moste men had. In whych respect he did before his last departynge downe from hence into Penbroke shire of speciall trust leave in my handes the eyght and nynth bookes of Virgilles Eneidos, by him translated into Englyshe verse. And promised to use all hys possible diligence for the finishing of the other three bookes then utterly unbegonne: Declarynge moreover unto me that hys verye mynde and purpose was not onely to prynt the former part agayne for reformation of some faultes overslypt upon the first impression, but also havyng finished the same to dedicate the whole worke unto your Lordship, whome he tooke for a speciall Patrone and frendly favorer bothe of hym and hys doings. Albeit, it pleased God to prevent hym by death so as he coulde not make an ende thereof: yet since he lyked to commit these two bookes into my handes onely. The foarce of death shall not be able through my default to make hys worke dye: Neither shall hys good entent be frustrate in makyng your lordship the Patrone thereof (*2r).

The personal tone of Wightman's preface is suggestive. Phaer clearly took his *Eneidos* seriously enough to seek its official facilitation through the patronage of political ascendancy.

A university man himself, Sir Nicholas Bacon had certainly achieved prominence as outspoken Protestant parliamentarian during Phaer's last term as an MP in 1559. If, as Wightman declares, Phaer insisted on naming Bacon as patron, his public sympathies had changed from the dedication of the first edition to Queen Mary, "my moste soveraın good Ladie, and onely redoughted maistresse" (*Eneidos* 1558, A2r). But Phaer, like his earliest patron the Marquess of Winchester, assured himself of survival by staying in the political middle. Doubtless, after years of public life, he had also learned the most effective channels of political facilitation It comes as little surprise then that Phaer's, like many English families of the period, had daughters named Mary and Elizabeth.

Wightman takes personal pains to show how Phaer's *Eneidos* consumed his attentions to the end, declaring:

> Marie it should appeare by the two verses in the ende of this booke by hym translated upon his death bed the very day before he dyed, which he sent unto me subscribed with his left hand (the use of the right hande beyng taken away, through the hurte whereof he dyed) that he had gone so much further as those verses be in Virgilles tenth booke (*2v).

And those final verses? Wightman sees to it that they are printed at the conclusion for the sake of their appropriateness:

> Ech mans day stands prefixt, time short & swift with cureles bretche
> [I]s lotted al mankind, but by their deedes their fame to stretche
> That privilege vertue gives (Gg3r).

These lines from the *Aeneid* (10 479-81) were respectfully incorporated word-for-word by Thomas Twyne in completing the translation (Lally xxxviii). Phaer's linguistic expertise and power as cultural communicator lived on

Wightman's additional biographical detail of the untimely circumstance of Phaer's death is touching: the "hurte whereof he dyed" most likely involving a fall from a horse, as suggested in Sir Thomas Chaloner's "Epitaph on Thomas Phaer, physician:"

> Phaer, right worthy he of long drawn years,
> Alas, hath perished by untimely fate.
> The sword of Jove—and who shall 'scape his doom?—
> His blood hath spilt, hard fault of luckless gait. (Still 127)

But Phaer's life and work is difficult to condense into such elegiacs or to consider as biographically described by the posthumous praise of William Wightman or Barnabe Googe (25) or William Webbe (C3v-C4r) or others previously quoted. Thomas Churchyard, in his preface to

Skelton's *Works*, links Phaer to other English vernacular worthies such as Langland, Chaucer, and Surrey, declaring "And Phaer did hit the pricke, / In thinges he did translate." Clearly Phaer *was* on target and in the bull's-eye of English cultural communication in the early modern period.

And yet, according to medical historian George Frederic Still, even Phaer's memorial at Cilgerran is gone now along with the memorial brass he ordered and the very churchyard in which his body was interred. A tablet commemorating Phaer was erected at Cilgerran in 1986 (Cule 90-91). What remains is Phaer's multitalented contribution to learning and letters in his own time and ours, combining disciplines and translating them for popular edification In this transformative effort Phaer deserves the last word As spelled out in his preface to *The Boke of Chyldren*, he is determined "to shewe the remedyes that God hath created for the use of man to distrybute in Englysshe to them that are unlerned part of the treasure that is in other languages" (27). These "other languages" include the language of law, of Latin, of parliamentary debate, of folk belief, of medical inquiry, of the human body itself. And it is to that early modern language of medicine that we must turn in considering Phaer's seminal pediatrics text.

The Text

Thomas Phaer's *The Boke of Chyldren* appeared in 1544. The work was printed by Edward Whytchurche in one volume along with three other medical pieces Phaer's translation of Jehan Goeurot's *The Regiment of Lyfe*, *A goodly Bryefe Treatise of the Pestylence*, and *A Declaration of the Veynes*, both by Phaer The text was widely popular, and is listed as one of the thirteen "Medical best-sellers 1486–1604" in Paul Slack's essay on vernacular medical literature of Tudor England (248). During the sixteenth century, *The Regiment of Lyfe* was a most important title, and the volume is identified accordingly. But, from a medical and literary standpoint, it is *The Boke of Chyldren* that deserves precedence. In fact *The Boke of Chyldren* does precede the main text in Whytchurche's 1544 printing. In all subsequent editions, however, Phaer's *Boke of Chyldren* is last in the volume while the preface remains at the beginning. This seems appropriate, because the preface to *The Boke of Chyldren* is something of a populist manifesto in which Phaer sets forth his general terms, conditions, and preconceptions as medical-cultural communicator.

This book is set apart by its sense of specialization and by its precedent-setting "Englishness." Indeed Phaer's defense of the vernacular reads like a spirited offensive thrust. Like Phaer's other publications in medicine, law, and the classics, *The Boke of Chyldren* is also a cultural text that asserts English as a language suitable for learned consciousness. Herein Phaer displays a profound mobility of intellect which he transposes onto his text. By changing the language of original medical reportage to English, Phaer effectively changes medical practice. He localizes it, demystifies it, shares it with his countrymen for whom he was soon to sit as parliamentary representative. Phaer thus represents a significant social voice. The nature of the book's specialization is also significant in that it focuses premorbid attention on to a specific segment of the population hitherto ignored as a patient-group in its own right. This, in a period when early childhood diseases were usually fatal, makes *The Boke of Chyldren* an important original contribution; and its reprinting throughout the Tudor period in England certainly credits its popularity.

In their cultural assertiveness, authoritative certainty, and printed stability as "English" learning, Phaer's books both define and benefit from an incipient cultural nationalism. His use of the vernacular democratizes learning across disciplines where English is valorized as a means to cultural advancement and cultural definition. According to Linda Voigts in *Speculum*, by 1475 vernacular English was common and accepted, was "considered an appropriate medium for nearly every sort of university-derived scientific and medical writing" (817). She notes that after 1475 scholars can find "a full range of sophisticated university treatises—mostly on medicine and astronomy—in English-language manuscripts where Latin plays little or no role" (814). But Voigts describes a university and manuscript culture of elite learning. Phaer's milieu involves popular print. His is not the voice of one scholar speaking to other scholars Rather, he is an expert speaking to all, and his defensiveness indicates that his practice is not without opposition. Even if a current anti-English lobby was more perceived than real, Phaer's sharp tone certainly sets his project apart as distinctly English, Tudor, and contemporary. Besides, in matters of medical and scientific doctrine, sharp attacks on predecessors and adversaries were considered standard procedure as far back as Galen, as noted by Siegel in his volume on the work of the great classical physician.

Boyd Berry curiously attributes a measure of paranoia to Phaer, considering him as threatened within a milieu of Tudor social dislocation. He correctly refers to Phaer as a "linguistic nationalist" (566), but then goes on to trivialize the emerging power of print, declaring incredulously that Phaer "sees himself threatened merely for publishing a book" (568) However, the power of the printed word flexes remarkably in this early period of sectarian contention, vigorous publication, and information transferral. One might consider early print culture to be involved in an information struggle for people's minds In her richly informative study, *The Printing Press as an Agent of Change*, Elizabeth Eisenstein notes the power of print dissemination in addition to intellectual cross-fertilization and cultural exchange as afforded by printed texts in all their variety Clearly Phaer, broadcasting information in printed English as opposed to guarding it in specialized academic language, is very much a creature of print culture. And print, as the invention that actually advertises itself, advertises itself in unstable relation to its own vernacular. Hence "English" becomes a published national consciousness, a developing and capitalizing vernacular as argued by Benedict Anderson in *Imagined Communities*. Through print, readers perceive their cultural location. Phaer therefore must be considered one of the earliest and most committed "English" cultural authorities

Indeed *The Boke of Chyldren*, England's first pediatrics text, was preceded as a study only by Richard Jonas's translation of Roesslin's German obstetrics work, *The Byrth of Mankynde* (1540) Revised and reissued in 1545 by Thomas Raynold, this popular book contained prenatal and postpartum information for midwives Herein, Raynold too felt moved to defend the vernacular· "sume alledging that it is shame, and other sume that it is not mete ne syttyng such matter to be entreatyd of, soo playnely in our mother and vulgare langage" (Eccles, "Early Use of English for Midwiferies," 380). Thomas Phaer clearly knew the work (appropriating its section on "goggle eyes" for his own text), and had it in mind when he wrote his own more patient-specific *Boke of Chyldren* But Phaer's interest is non-obstetric, strictly postpartum, and more clearly focused on infant survival and quality of life. As Phaer himself puts it, children deserve specialized medical attention "by reason of theyr weakenesse" (31). His book is "of" children, speaks to their needs and addresses their particular medical concerns.

Phaer knows that his text is breaking cultural ground in its topic and in its use of English. Such understanding informs his defensive tone at the outset of the preface where he seeks to deflect interpretive criticism. His subjective, parenthetical interventions here and throughout show him to be self-conscious, critically aware, and well schooled in argument And his opening series of infinitives makes clear his populist commitment:

> My purpose is here to do them good that have moost nede, that
> is to say chyldren, and to shewe the remedyes that God hath
> created for the use of man to distrybute in Englysshe to them
> that are unlerned part of the treasure that is in other languages,
> to provoke them that are of better lernyng to utter theyr knowl-
> ege in suche lyke attemptes, finallye to declare that to the use of
> many which ought not to be secrete for lucre of a fewe (27).

The tone is learned, virtuous, and generous. Phaer takes direct aim at received notions of medical treatment and patient care and determines to change them through clearly reported English information.

Good health and medical service have been precious commodities since antiquity, and wealthy patients have always been prepared to pay for recondite advice and expensive treatment. Physicians historically have relished an image of themselves as mysterious, private healers, as advisors privy to secret knowledge, as scholars communicating in a special language. Phaer, however, attacks this cherished image directly.

> Why grutche they phisik to come forth in Englysshe? wolde they
> have no man to knowe but onely they? Or what make they
> themselves? Marchauntes of our lyves and deathes, that wee
> shulde buy our health only of them and at theyr pryces? No
> good phisicion is of that mynde (27)

His concluding imperative is direct and critical, unlike that of anonymous forebears prior to the invention of printing. Audrey Eccles quotes the purpose of some early English translators directly: "be cause he had a gud frend that under stod no latyn;" and, "I wyl wright of women prevy sekenes the helpyng and that oon woman may helpe a nother" ("The Reading Public," 144, 145) Such justification is as marginalized as it is touching. Contained within localized premodern manuscripts, such attempts at distributing knowledge remain unapprehended. As a publishing authority of the English Renaissance, however, Phaer couches his criticism in more social terms, in terms of mass-communicated culture through printing. His text is for everyone

But *The Boke of Chyldren*, like all literature, is also keyed to underlying material conditions which determine the logic of its specific discourse. The book exists as the material product of a sixteenth-century mind identified as Thomas Phaer. This mind was nourished by material conditions of upbringing, education, conflict, and lived experience. It produced extant written texts, of which *The Boke of Chyldren* is but one. Indeed, as political-textual theorist Christopher Hampton puts it, "the mind's products, its systems of thought, its ideas, its propositions, are *themselves* material products" (17). And thus it is for Phaer's book on children, along with the mental and cultural preconditions that both shape and inform it: English nationalism under Henry VIII; professional training at the inns of court; the internationalism of university life in early modern Europe; widespread infant and childhood mortality; authoritative concern about surgery and midwifery; a burgeoning sense of post-Reformation criticism; ancient folk wisdom and inchoate empiricism; political instability perhaps coupled with a deeply-felt "save-the-children" sense of conservative social responsibility.

Phaer, too, is socially determined, is clearly the product of his surrounding social context. Biographical material describes the author as middle class, well educated, and politic. He is clearly in touch with the social and political vicissitudes of his day, perhaps explaining his various public positions and responsibilities. Phaer's was a cultural establishment at once respected but also under social stress. Indeed *any* establishment was threatened in the Reformation and Counter-Reformation climate of early Tudor England. Hence, perhaps, Phaer's politic decampment to Wales, to its relatively safe marginality, its rural complacency, its fundamentally Tudor allegiance. And his medical consciousness was also determined in no small bit by a social order reliant on native English rather than Latin or even Welsh. This period in England charted a cultural shift from a priest class chanting Latin repetitions to Protestant vernacular texts having to do with thesis and analysis.

The rise of the printed text nourished an unprecedented instructional culture, a culture informed by humanist texts such as *The Boke of the Governor* but also by a myriad of more popular texts on religious discipline, folk and medical remedies, and occult events. These books— and *The Boke of Chyldren* represents a significant progressive example— were informative, not catechismal, vernacular, not Latin, social, not sacred. Such changes in emphasis and approach signal changes in the general social orientations of academic life that informed Thomas Phaer: from the analogical to the empirical, from a medieval love of patterning to a Renaissance discourse of exploration and discovery. In *Science and the Secrets of Nature*, William Eamon accurately charts the direction of contemporary informational culture:

> The concern with the material needs of everyday life, the emphasis upon hands-on experience, the confirmation of the greater efficacy of technology over the sacred, and the availability of self-education through reading—all these forces contributed to a

growing awareness that humanity's lot could be bettered, not by magic, cunning, or the grace of God, but by knowing "how to" (133).

The Boke of Chyldren is a medical document that attempts to communicate "how to" within the complicated cultural positions of sixteenth-century England In effect, the document reaches out to touch and inform those who read it The specific remedies it rehearses may often be superstitious in nature, indeed ludicrous in conception, but they make sense to Phaer and his readership in terms of an overarching Galenic teleology, a holistic view of the world and of everything divinely provided in the world—plant, mineral, animal, human. Clearly a student of Galen, Phaer would agree with the great authority that the best physician must also be a philosopher, a philosopher unifying reason with experimentation and learning. Phaer's words signify a learned relationship, an exchange of social views and practice with the practice of his inquiring readers Hereby, the book communicates material realities that precede language: childhood development, disease, and well-being—indeed quality of infant life as advised through contemporary remedies and through the Galenic synthesis of ancient authorities such as Hippocrates, Plato, and Aristotle.

The Boke of Chyldren thus tries to communicate specialized medical advice for children. It manifests a variety of rhetorical strategies including direct advice, authoritative appeal, and personal observation. But it operates at a level beyond M. J. Tucker's observation of pseudoscience and enthusiasm for systematization (235). Language, here, is a vehicle to inform. And it informs through a certain "style" of discourse, a style that precedes later scientific rigor through its appeal to authority Indeed the book's own tiny emergence, embedded as it is within the volume of *The Regiment of Lyfe*, signals it as attached to received authority and yet clearly set apart from it with its own title and specific focus on the subject of children. That the book manifests a "grammar" of its own popular authority is quickly evidenced by Phaer's appeal to vernacular authorities such as "prynce" Galen (27) and "Kyng" Avicenna (28) as royally compassionate authorities on medical doctrine. It is then but one metaphorical step more to quote Christ from the Sermon on the Mount. And Phaer immediately does so for the purpose of emotional compulsion and authority in his readership, a readership which he presumes to be Christian, literate, activist, and, above all, concerned.

Phaer decries secrecy or diffidence as "a detestable thyng in any godlye science," but as especially "damnable and devylyshe" (28) in relation to medical knowledge. And yet he appeals often to emotional associations of folk practicality, herbal lore, and contemporary esotericism. Concerning paradoxical cold and heat, Phaer notes a "wounderfulle secrete of nature" (43), signaling appeal to the then-current books of "secrets," a popular literature characterized by Eamon as "traditional lore concerning the occult properties of plants, stones, and animals, along with miscellaneous craft and medicinal recipes, alchemical formulas, and 'experiments' to produce marvelous effects through magic" (16). Phaer's emotional, cultural, and preempirical approach represents a contemporary medical discursive practice oriented toward satisfaction. He incorporates a wide-ranging discursive practice having to do with a whole group of functions of observation, record, interrogation, suggestion, criticism, religious appeal, and overt condemnation, that passes for medical discourse in his time and ours. Phaer provides advice for contemporary English parents, but the book suggests that he listened to them too as many of the remedies are folk-based and naive. Ever the populist, Phaer himself hopes that his book will "be redde of as many as wold" (28).

But the book is still a special kind of text, a medical text that conveys its information through authoritative textual appeal As Phaer insists, "the very bare texte shal be there alleged ... folowyng therein not onlye the famous and excellent authours of antiquitye, but also the men of hyghe learnynge nowe of oure dayes" (28-29). A structure of specific interventions makes *The Boke of Chyldren* something of a remedy book, but it is certainly beyond the loose medical *receptaria* of astrological computations, secrets, humoral theory, uroscopy, charms, prayers, cupping, and various ritual actions having to do with the time of year or nature of the patient. It casts off Latin only to return to Latinate structures that make it a book of real medical inquiry. As Linda Voigts explains in *Editing Texts in the History of Science and Medicine·*

> Fourteenth-century prose was essentially paratactic with a high number of coordinating conjunctions and a structure based on repetition, parallelism, balance and contrast, in short, a language quite different from Latin. Yet, by 1500 English had adopted many of the hypotactic capacities of Latin; the fifteenth century saw the introduction of a number of subordinating conjunctions in English and a growth of use of a variety of subordinating devices that encourage qualification and signal relationships of cause and doubt (53-54).

Just so. Phaer's sixteenth-century prose appeals to authority in the widely-incorporative Galenic manner, but it also goes its own way in terms of contemporary contingency, stylistics, inquiry, and exploration.

Phaer concludes his preface by defending the previous edition of *The Regiment of Lyfe*, and "the straunge ingrediens wherof it often treateth" (29). He makes no apology for responsible innovation and expansion of knowledge. Moreover, he claims to have simplified matters in *The Boke of Chyldren* by focusing on local herbs and remedies "as may be easelye gotten" (29), and does not hesitate to refer readers back to appropriate passages in *The Regiment of Lyfe*. Such "simplification" reminds Phaer of his stated purpose to translate and perfectly declare the nature of "Simples"—uncompounded medicaments—of the later Middle Ages, with all of their interconnections and signatures concerning plants, roots, seeds, and their various interactions. Many contemporary printed herbals existed (Arber, Appendix I), but none of them in English Indeed Phaer is insistent on the point.

> I hope to see the tyme whan the nature of Simples (whych have ben hytherto incrediblie corrupted) shal be redde in Englysshe as in other languages: that is to saye, the perfecte declaration of the qualities of herbes, seedes, rootes, trees, and of all commodities that are here amongest us, shal be earnestely and trulye declared in oure owne natyve speche (29)

Citing the great classical herbalist Dioscorides throughout his text, Phaer must have been pleased to see William Turner's English herbals appear within a few years in 1548 and 1551. And, like Phaer, Turner is defensive on his use of the vernacular, pleading the necessity of English surgeons and apothecaries, and declaring of himself "then am I no hinderer writing unto the English my countrymen an English herbal" (*New Herball* 216). As previously noted, both shared a Commons sitting as well as a distinct commitment to the popularizing nature of the English language.

Phaer's *Boke of Chyldren* contains much "simple" advice—literally, figuratively, herbally, and medically. And, in a clever, telling irony, Phaer dedicates his own "simple power" (29) to the medical common good. His sense of simplicity comprises a wide knowledge of herbal combinations, but also focuses his readers on medical information in their own vernacular—an assignment that is at once simple and, in its own time, very complex Phaer combines humanist learning through classical authorities such as Dioscorides and Galen, but he also remains sensitive to folk and household cures. His project effectively synthesizes contemporary science and popular advice As stated before, by presenting medical information in the vernacular and insisting on its local familiarization, Phaer effectively changes the way in which medicine is performed and reported

Phaer's is a physician's concern with complex combinations of herbs, chemicals, behavioral restrictions, and appropriate actions to facilitate the comfort and well-being of his patient group—in this case, children. His focus suggests that children, as an identifiable group, were a valuable consideration in early modern England, a consideration beyond the behavioral, picturesque, or ornamental notions of Ariès's study in *Centuries of Childhood*. One might usefully compare Ariès's esthetic observation, "the appearance of the portrait of the dead child in the sixteenth century accordingly marked a very important moment in the history of feelings" (40), with Phaer's more practical materialist consideration of live, healthy children and their medical requirements

In Phaer's view and practice, the child is a weak, undeveloped member of the populace requiring physical attention specific to needs. His concern runs counter to Ariès's notions of emotional indifference. To Phaer, children are special, important, different from adults, and deserving of care Such attention begins with a specialized form of nourishment in breast-feeding and a necessity for much sleep This concern explains Phaer's early focus on nursing in *The Boke of Chyldren* along with the many attendant dietary and behavioral restrictions involved. Phaer reports a practice of intensive medical attention, attention sensitive to the notions argued in opposition to Ariès by Linda Pollock in *Forgotten Children*. children, then and now, are rapidly developmental, playful, in need of protection, care, guidance, and financial support (Pollock 98). Parents, then and now, attempt usually to attend to such provisions.

Raising children is considered as a medical, moral, and social regimen, inculcating a discipline to facilitate encounters with early childhood diseases, and to allow the child to pass into prepubescent life. Indeed, having achieved the age of six or seven, the child had a strong chance of surviving into adulthood and contributing to society But children were not customarily ignored or abused up to that point as argued by Ariès and de Mause. Rather, as Hanawalt notes (61), even unknown and presumably abandoned children found dead in the period received burial at the expense of the wealthier members of the local parish. Citing contemporary diarist accounts, Pollock (124–28) is especially revealing on the extent of parental anxiety over childhood illness and death in the period.

Presumably, such concern informs Phaer's insistence on the moral and nutritional qualities of the nurse. His best-case scenario would involve the breast-feeding nourishment of a loving mother. But, failing that, the nurse shall be, in Phaer's words, "sobre, honest and chaste, well fourmed, amyable and chearefull, so that she maye accustome the infant unto myrthe, ... an honest woman (suche as had a man chylde last afore is best)" (33). The paternalist physican must always, it seems, assert masculinity as a moral good running counter to feminine laxity A man of his time, Phaer affirms such sexist social responsibility and medical intervention, as in the treatment of stiff joints: "whyche thynge procedeth many tymes of colde as whan a chylde is founde in the frost or in the strete, caste awaye by a wycked mother" (43). But, to his credit, Phaer does distance himself from his own prejudice in the clause that follows, declaring, "I am not ignorant that it may procede of manye other causes " However holistic and socially concerned, Phaer characteristically returns quickly to the stable ground of specific diagnosis and remedy

Phaer's medical approach is clearly post-obstetric and pre-etiquette, having little in common with the many devotional and catechismal books for children in sixteenth- and seventeenth-century England detailed by Demers, or with the precepts about table manners found in *The Babees Book* (c.1475) edited by Furnivall. Moreover, Phaer begins specifically by departing from the many complicated manual things "pertaynyng onely to the office of a mydwyfe" (31). He considers such things as "the beinge in the wombe, the tyme of procedyng, the maner of the byrth, the byndyng of the navyll, settynge of the membres, lavatories, unctions, swathinges, and entreatementes" (31) to be matters of extreme modesty to be attended only by women.

A contemporary network of experienced mothers and cunning women no doubt provided frontline care for children generally, although midwives in England had been officially regulated along with physicians and surgeons since the time of Henry VIII. Indeed prospective midwives had to swear an oath before a Bishop's Court, abjuring witchcraft, promising never to substitute or interfere with newborns, and learning the official sacraments for infant baptism. In *Midwives in History and Society*, Towler and Bramall quote from the oath sworn on August 26, 1567 by midwife Eleanor Pead (56–57). Quite apart from Ariès's sense of indifference and Phaer's sense of modesty, childbirth was certainly important enough to catch the regulative attention of official Tudor policy.

And Tudor policy was gendered male. Indeed the complicated behavioral and dietary prohibitions to which nursing women were put only serve to clarify the systematic paternalistic control of the period. Male physicians exercised overwhelming control over regulation of medical public policy and over women's bodies as well. As argued by Jean Donnison in *Midwives and Medical Men*, the period historically charts a course of gradual loss of female influence through male medical ascendancy. Masculine authority seems nervously intrusive in the matter of childbirth and early infant care, a nervousness perhaps signaled later in Phaer's document when considering "swellynge of the coddes" (70) or scrotum. Herein sexual matters are of concern to Phaer, drawing him back to his original concern with breast-feeding as he forbids hemlock plasters and their adverse effect on secondary sexual characteristics: "set no playster to the stones wherin hymlocke entereth, for it wyll depryve them for ever of their growynge; and not only them but the brestes of wenches whan they be annoynted therewyth" (71). Sex and gender and power, as always, are implicated in medical prescription. As in the medical politics of the period, womanly attention to children is reconfigured within Phaer's text to dictate a new medical esthetic having to do with instruction, advice, and compliance.

This new medical esthetic, however, continues its assertion of received physical comparisons, especially the then current doctrine of signatures which suggested that God had set a clue to the medical nature of every plant in terms of its outward appearance. For the purposes of treatment, appearances were of utmost importance. Consider Phaer's own analogical reasoning for warming chilled limbs in cold water:

> When an apple or a pere is frosen in the wynter, sette it to the fyer and it is destroyed; but yf ye putte it into colde water, it shall as well endure as it dyd afore; whereby it doth appere that the water resolveth colde better wyth his moysture than the fyer can do by reason of hys heate (44).

And yet Phaer takes the middle way, declaring, "when a yonge chylde is so taken with a colde, I esteme it best for to bathe the bodye in luke warme water" (44). He exercises the mediating judgment of a wise experienced physician. Still, Phaer sees the wisdom of treating the falling sickness, "called in the Greke tonge epilepsia" (40) with "the muscle of the oke" (41) or with a decoction of linden tree blossoms. The effect: associative strength to keep the patient from falling. As Phaer authoritatively notes of the linden, "it is a tree called in Latyne tilia, the same wherof they make ropes and halters of the barke" (41). Presumably, rope and halter associations with the linden will combine with the strength of the oak to sustain the patient against "falling." A similar line of reasoning informs the prescription of "oyntment of an hares galle" to "amende deafnesse" (50), or the "braynes of an hare" (51) to alleviate teething pains. The size of rabbit ears and teeth, along with benign animal associations, seem to be medicinally vital to a Renaissance physician seeking appropriate cause and effect in medications.

But Phaer is also providing practical advice in the manner of a country doctor. To Phaer, an "outragious syckenes" (54) such as quinsy or swollen lymph glands calls for an outrageous cure, so he falls back upon the appropriateness of preparing "a swallowe brent wyth fethers and all and myxte wyth honye, whereof the pacient must *swallowe* downe a lytle" (54; my emphasis). Here, the word "swallow" seems to be signifier, signified, and remedy. Also prescribed. "the pouder of the chyldes dunge to the chyld" (54). This, doubtless on the reasoning that what has passed once may easily pass again. Bear in mind, however, that Phaer was a long way removed from previous antirational theorists such as Nicholas of Poland who, in the latter half of the thirteenth century, posited that God had implanted special healing virtues in obnoxious things such as snakes, lizards, and frogs (Siraisi 33). Presumably, this explains Phaer's reliance instead on such exquisite medicaments as dove's dung, hare's brains, or "the lycour that yssueth out of shepes clawes or gootes clawes, hette in the fyer" (69). Phaer also sees the appropriateness of treating chafed feet with "fragmentes of shomakers lether" (67), at the same time as he appears to anticipate mold-based antibiotics in his reliance on certain mushrooms mixed in hot drink as a remedy for quinsy (54–55). As well, in the case of the common cold, Phaer advocates postural drainage of mucus as follows·

> holdynge downe his head that the reumes maye issue, for by that meanes the cause of the cough shall ren out of hys mouth and avoyde the chylde of many noughtie and slymy humours; whyche done, many tymes the paciente amendeth wythout any further helpe of medicine (55).

Such a procedure, combined with warm, sweet drinks, anticipates by some four hundred and fifty years the conclusion published in the *Journal of the American Medical Association* (May 5, 1993): "No good evidence has demonstrated the effectiveness of over-the-counter cold medications in preschool children" (Smith and Feldman 2263). Phaer's practical procedures seem well-suited to his status as both country doctor and intellectually curious physician

And yet Phaer's document asserts scholastic opinion almost as much as practical intervention. This was the standard procedure of the Renaissance physician, schooled in analyses often with legal or theological emphasis Throughout, he signals his learning as text-based in holistic Galenic terms. Indeed, Phaer seems to rely often upon the authority of naming terms, as in the section on "canker in the mouthe":

> I knowe that the Greekes and auncente Latynes gyve other names unto this dysease, as in callynge it an ulcer, other whyles aphthe, nome, carcinoma, and lyke, whiche are al in Englyshe knowen by the name of canker in the mouthe (52).

Likewise, in describing "small pockes and measylles," Phaer assures his readers of the general etymology and prevalence of these common childhood diseases at the same time as he wisely counsels, "The best and most sure helpe in this case is not to meddle wyth any kynde of medicines, but to let nature woorke her operation" (68).

In the section on "scabbynesse and ytche," Phaer challenges practitioners too reliant on the terminology of Dioscorides, especially Vigo, the renowned Italian surgeon. Phaer corrects such misguided medical interventionists by correcting their misuse of terminology, alleging of Vigo's error.

> It was for nothynge els but lacke of the tonges, which faulte is not to be so hyghly rebuked in a man of his studye, applyinge himselfe more to the practyse of surgerye and to handye operation, wherein indede he was nere incomparable, than he dyd to search the varyaunce of tonges (47)

Clearly, the physician's learned analysis of terms is to be privileged over the surgeon's mechanistic approach. Physical diagnosis can be more effective than physical intervention. The physician can "tell" the problem, can name it and thus prescribe the recondite physical measures and medicaments to be exercised and taken. In so doing, the physician registers the patient as part of a whole whose suffering is not unique, whose recovery is certainly possible.

At all points, the physician's stature as authority, and position within learned gentility, is to be emphasized. Physicians were philosophically trained in classical and recondite texts, texts such as Galen's that presumably held *all* the pertinent answers. As a gentle scholar with connections at the inns of court or a university college, Phaer relies on preconceptions of class to accentuate his prescriptions. Surgeons—even celebrated and scholarly ones such as Vigo, or Phaer's own compatriot, Thomas Vicary—are basically tradesmen involved in "handye operation." In using such terms, Phaer demurely wafts his learning over the Greek etymological roots of surgery, as stated directly a few years later in Vicary's own *Anatomie of the Bodie of Man* (1548)· "Surgerie is derived oute of these wordes, *Apo tes chiros, cai tou ergou*, that is too bee understanded, A hand working" (12) The surgeons of early modern Europe, especially in England, were working-class and thus negligible as medical authorities, although historian Vivian Nutton argues otherwise in a suggestive essay entitled "Humanist Surgery." A cultivated image of gentle, learned trustworthiness ensured the physicians their position of preeminence.

The founding of the Royal College of Physicians in London (1518) accorded significant privilege and power to theoretical scholastics, further degrading the practical knowledge of physiology that surgeons had gained over the course of the previous two centuries on battlefields and at bedsides. While physicians enjoyed genteel university associations, surgeons were returned to the civic organization of the trade guilds. Just as apothecaries were usually associated with the grocers' and spicers' companies, the surgeons were merged with the barbers' guild by act of Parliament in 1540. Previous English kings such as Edward I, Edward III, and Henry V had relied on an army of respectable surgeons in their foreign wars. But Henry VIII preferred cold-war détente with the Continent and privileged university contemplations of physic over the practical interventions of surgery. A new age of doctrine and dispute suppressed the practicalities of bloody surgical intervention while emphasizing scholastic supposition and debate.

By the early middle part of the sixteenth century in England, an explosion of printed books also contributed to the enhanced privilege of scholastic authority Phaer, with his published opinion on law, medicine, and the classics, takes his place of authority always within terms of text and interpretation. And although speculative theory can often deflect attention from clear observation of issues, Phaer maintains his observations in *The Boke of Chyldren* clearly on his subject· the health and well-being of children At all points, he considers children—their predisposition to disease, their physical weakness, their lack of agency—to be a special group in medical consideration and treatment And this opinion is unprecedented

To be sure, Phaer engages in rhetorical self-references near the conclusion of his monograph, sending his reader back to pertinent sections of *The Boke of Chyldren* to validate assertions made. But, in many ways, his job has been completed in the very publication of his treatise. It offers little in the way of powerful empirical inquiry, although his methods seem poised confidently on the cusp. Nor does Phaer advance any fully recognizable scientific approach, any consistent methodology, or even a linked series of possibilities. Rather, he advances an "English" text, a text that allows common readers to consider the material, medical status of children. Phaer concludes: "Neyther desyre I any lenger to lyve than I wil employe my studyes to the honoure of God and profyt of the weale publike" (77). Assuredly this little book—*the* English textbook on pediatrics into the next century—did profit the "weale publike" by allowing Englishmen to think about early childhood diseases in their own language and to suggest that they might profitably take measures against those diseases. The text that follows is edited in the hopes of providing a clearer historicized understanding of early English medicine and its published communication.

Thomas Phaer
and
The Boke of Chyldren (1544)

THE PREFACE TO THE BOKE OF CHYLDREN

Althoughe (as I doubt not) everye good man wil enterpret this worke to none other ende but to be for the comforte of them that are diseased, and wyl esteme no lesse of me by whom they profyte, than they wyll be glad to receyve the benefites. Yet, for as moche as it is impossyble to avoyd the teeth of malicyous envye, I thought it not unnecessary to prevent the furyes of some, whiche are ever gnawynge and bytynge upon them that further any godlye scyences. To those I protest, that in al my studyes I never entended nor yet do entend to satisfy the mindes of any suche pikfaultes (which wyll do nothyng but detract and judge others, snuffyng at all that offendeth the noses of theyr momyshe affections, howsoever laudable it be otherwayes). But my purpose is here to do them good that have moost nede, that is to say chyldren, and to shewe the remedyes that God hath created for the use of man to distrybute in Englysshe to them that are unlerned part of the treasure that is in other languages, to provoke them that are of better lernyng to utter theyr knowlege in suche lyke attemptes, finallye to declare that to the use of many which ought not to be secrete for lucre of a fewe, and to communicat the frute of my labours to them that wyl gently and thankefully receyve them; which yf any be so proud or supercilious that they immediatly wil despise, I shall frendly desyre them, wyth the wordes of Horace. *Quod si meliora nouisti, Candidus imparti, si non, his utere mecum.* If they know better, let us have parte; if they do not, why repyne they at me? why condemne they the thing that they cannot amend? or if they can, why dissimule they theyr connyng? how longe wold they have the people ignoraunt? why grutche they phisik to come forth in Englysshe? wolde they have no man to knowe but onely they? Or what make they themselves? Marchauntes of our lyves and deathes, that wee shulde buy our health only of them and at theyr pryces? No good phisicion is of that mynde. For yf Galene the prynce of thys arte beinge a

Grecian, wrote in the Greke, Kyng Avicenne of Arabie in the speche of hys Arabyans; yf Plinius, Celsus, Serenus, and other of the Latynes wrote to the people in the Latyne tonge, Marsilius Ficinus (whome all men assente to be singularly learned) disdayned not to wryte in the language of Italy. Generally, yf the entent of al that ever set forth any noble studye have ben to be redde of as many as wold, what reason is it that we shuld huther muther[1] here amonge a fewe the thynge that was made to be common unto all? Chryst sayeth: No man lyghteth a candle to cover it with a bushell, but setteth it to serve every mans nede.[2] And these go about not only to cover it when it is lyghted, but to quench it afore it be kendled (if they myght by malyce); whych as it is a detestable thyng in any godlye science, so me thynketh in thys so necessarye an arte it is excedynge damnable and devylyshe to debarre the fruycion of so inestimable benefytes which our heavenlye father hath prepared for oure comfort and innumerable uses, wherwyth he hath armed oure impotent nature agaynst the assaultes of so many sycknesses; wherby his infynyte mercye and aboundaunte goodnesse is in nothynge els more apparauntly confessed by the which benefites; as it wer with moost sensible argumentes spoken out of heven, he constrayneth us to thinke upon our own weakenesse, and to knowledge that in all fleshe is nothynge but myserie, siknesse, sorowes, synne, affliction, and deathe, no not so moche strengthe as by our owne power to relyeve one member of our bodyes diseased. As for the knoweledge of medicines, comfort of herbes, mayntenaunce of healthe, prosperytie, and lyfe, they be hys benefyttes, and procede of hym, to the ende that we shulde in common helpe one an other, and so lyve togyther in hys lawes and commaundementes; in the which doyng we shal declare oureselves to have woorthelye employed them, and as frutefull servauntes be liberallye rewarded. Otherwyse, undoutedly the talente whyche we have hydden shall be dygged up and distributed to them that shall be more diligent: a terrible confusion afore so hye a justyce, and at such a court, where no wager of lawe shall be taken, no proctoure lymytted to defende the cause, none exception allowed to reprove the wytnes, no councel admytted to qualifye the gloses; the very bare texte shal be there alleged: *Cur non posuisti talentum in fenus*? Whye haste thou not bestowed my talente to the

---

[1] i.e., hugger mugger; to maintain secrecy.
[2] From the Sermon on the Mount; see Matthew 5:15, Mark 4:21, Luke 8:16. Phaer is perhaps relying on memory or on his own interpreted understanding, as the line does not correspond exactly to Tyndale's translation.

vauntage?[3] These and suche other examples have enforced me, beynge oftentymes exercysed in the studye of phisike, to deryve out of the purest fountaynes of the same facultye such holsome remedyes as are most approved to the consolation of them that are afflycted, as farre as God hathe gyven me understandyng to perceyve; folowyng therein not onlye the famous and excellent authours of antiquitye, but also the men of hyghe learnynge nowe of oure dayes, as Manardus, Fuchsius, Ruellius, Musa, Campegius, Sebastyan of Austryke, Otho Brunfelsius, Leonellus, etc. wyth dyvers other for myne oportunitye, not omyttynge also the good and sure experimentes that are founde profitable by the daylye practyse.

And whereas in the *Regyment of Lyfe*, whyche I translated out of the Frenche tonge, it hath appered to some more curyouse than nedeth, by reason of the straunge ingrediens wherof it often treateth, ye shal knowe that I have in manye places amplyfyed the same wyth suche common thynges as may be easelye gotten, to satysfie the myndes of them that were offended; or els considering that there is no moneye so precious as helth, I wold thinke no spice too dere for mayntenauns therof. Notwythstandynge, I hope to see the tyme whan the nature of Simples (whych have ben hytherto incrediblie corrupted) shal be redde in Englysshe as in other languages: that is to saye, the perfecte declaration of the qualities of herbes, seedes, rootes, trees, and of all commodities that are here amongest us, shal be earnestely and trulye declared in oure owne natyve speche by the grace of God. To the whyche I trust al lerned men (havyng a zele to the common wealth) wyll apply theyr diligent industries. Surely for my parte, I shal never cease, during my breath, to bestowe my labour to the furtheraunce of it (tylle it come to passe) even to the uttermoste of my simple power. Thus fare ye well gentle reders

Londini, mense maii.
1544.

---

[3] Again, loosely taken from the Parable of the Talents, see Matthew 25 14–30

THE BOKE OF CHYLDREN

To begyn a treatyse of the cure of chyldren, it shoulde seme expedyent that we shuld declare somewhat of the princyples, as of the generacion, the beinge in the wombe, the tyme of procedyng, the maner of the byrth, the byndyng of the navyll, settynge of the membres, lavatories, unctions, swathinges, and entreatementes, with the circumstaunces of these and many other, which if I shuld reherce in particles, it wolde requyre both a longer tyme and encrease into a greater volume. But forasmoch as the moost of these thynges are verye tryte and manifest, some pertaynyng onely to the office of a mydwyfe, other for the reverence of the matter, not mete to be disclosed to every vyle person: I entende in this boke to let them all passe, and to treate onely of the thynges necessarye, as to remove the sycknesses wherwith the tender babes are oftentymes afflycted and desolate of remedye, for so moche as manye do suppose that there is no cure to be ministred unto them by reason of theyr weakenesse. And by that vayne opinion, yea rather by a foolyshe feare, they forsake manye that myght be well recovered, as it shall appeare by the grace of God hereafter in thys lytle treatyse when we come to declaration of the medicynes In the meane season for confinitye[4] of the matter, I entend to wryte somwhat of the nource, and of the mylke, wyth the qualities and complexions of the same, for in that consysteth the chefe poynt and summe, not onelye of the mayntenaunce of health, but also of the fourmyng or infectyng eyther of the wytte or maners, as the Poet Virgill, when he wolde descrybe an uncurteys, churlysh, and a rude condishioned tyraunt, dydde attrybute the faulte unto the gyver of the mylke, as in sayinge thus:

Nec tibi diua parens, generis nec Dardanus author,

---

[4] The *OED* credits Phaer with first use of "confinity," declaring the term rare or obsolete "The position of bordering on something else, neighbourhood, contiguity, adjacency"

> *Perfide, sed duris genuit te cautibus horrens*
> *Caucasus, hircanaeque admorunt vbera tigres.*[5]

For that devyne Poet, being throughly expert in the privities of nature, understode ryght well how great an alteration everye thynge taketh of the humoure, by the whych it hathe his alyment and nouryshyng in the youth; which thyng also was consydred and alleged of manye wyse Philosophers: Plato, Theophrastus, Xenophon, Aristotle, and Plinie, who dydde all ascrybe unto the nourcement as moche effect or more, as to the generacyon.

And Phavorinus the Philosopher (as wryteth Aulus Gellius)[6] affirmeth that if lambes be nouryshed with the milke of gootes, they shall have course wolle lyke the heere of gootes: and yf kyddes in lyke maner sucke upon shepe, the heere of them shal be softe lyke woll. Wherby it doth appeare that the mylke and nouryshyng hath a marveylous effecte in chaungyng the complexion, as we see lykewyse in herbes and in plantes, for let the seede or ympes[7] be never so good and pure, yet yf they be put into an unkynde earth or watred with a noughty and unholsome humour, eyther they come not up at all, or els they wyll degenerate and turne out of theyr kynde, so that scarse it may appeare from whence they have ben taken, accordynge to the verse:

> *Pomaque degenerant, succos oblita priores.*[8]

Wherfore as it is agreing to nature so is it also necessary and comly

---

[5] These lines from the *Aeneid* are translated thus by Phaer (Lally 83):

> No goddesse never was thy dame, nor thou of Dardans kinde
> Thou traitor wretche, but under rocks and mountaines rough unkinde
> Thou were begot, some brood thou art of beast or monster wilde,
> Some Tigres thee did nurse, and gave to thee their milke unmilde.
> (*Eneidos*, 4. 395–98)

Compare them with Christopher Marlowe's rigorous rendition some thirty years later:

> Thy mother was no Goddess, perjur'd man,
> Nor Dardanus the author of thy stock;
> But thou art sprung from Scythian Caucasus,
> And tigers of Hyrcania gave thee suck.
> (*Dido Queen of Carthage*, 5.1.156–59)

[6] The passage occurs in Gellius's *Noctes Atticæ*, vol. 2, bk. 12, chap. 1: "Dissertation of the philosopher Favorinus, in which he persuaded a lady of rank to suckle her child herself, and not to employ nurses."

[7] cuttings.

[8] The line is from Virgil's *Georgics*, 2.1.59: "Apples dwindle, forgetting their former savor."

for the owne mother to nource the owne child. Whyche yf it maye be done, it shall be moost commendable and holsome; yf not ye must be well advysed in takyng of a nource not of yll complexion and of worse maners, but suche as shall be sobre, honest and chaste, well fourmed, amyable and chearefull, so that she maye accustome the infant unto myrthe, no dronkarde, vycyous nor sluttysshe, for suche corrupteth the nature of the chylde. But an honest woman (suche as had a man chylde last afore is best) not within two monethes after her delyveraunce, nor approchynge nere unto her tyme agayne. These thynges ought to be consydred of every wyse person that wyll set theyr chyldren out to nource.

Moreover, it is good to loke upon the mylke, and to see whether it be thycke and grosse or too moche thynne and watrye, blackysshe or blewe, or enclynyng to reddnesse or yelowe, for all suche are unnaturall and evyll. Lykewyse when ye taste it in youre mouthe, yf it be eyther bytter, salte, or soure, ye may well perceyve it is unholsome

That mylke is good that is whyte and sweete, and when ye droppe it on your nayle, and do move your fynger, neyther fleteth abrode at every stering nor wyll hange faste upon your nayle when ye turne it downeward; but that whyche is betwene bothe is best.[9]

Sometyme it chaunceth that the mylke wasteth, so that the nource can not have sufficient to susteyne the child, for the which I wyl declare remedyes, leavynge out the causes for brevitie of tyme.

Remedyes appropriate to the encreasyng of mylke in the brestes.

Parsneppe rootes and fenelle rootes, sodden in broth of chyckens and afterward eaten wyth a lyttle fressh butter, maketh encrease of mylke within the brestes.

---

[9] To check for consistency of the milk, this "nail test" was still performed well into the twentieth century. In Jonas's 1540 translation of *The Byrth of Mankynde* (which Phaer follows closely throughout this early section on nursing), Roesslin reports

> That mylke is beste and moste to be chosen of the whiche a drop beynge mylked softely on the nail of the thombe, holdyng your fynger styll, it rolleth not of[f] neyther flytteth abrode; but yf ye move your hand a lyttell it will slyde of[f] by and by (O4v-P1r)

According to Ruhrah (158), the procedure may have originated with Soranus of Ephesus (98-138 AD), an early medical authority on a wide range of topics including obstetrics and midwifery.

An other.
The pouder of earth wormes, dryed and dronken in the brothe of a neates[10] tonge, is a singuler experiment for the same intent.

Also the broth of an olde cocke, wyth myntes, cynamome and maces.

Ryse also, sodden in cowes mylke wyth the cromes of whyte breed, fenel seede in pouder, and a lytle sugre, is excedyng good.

An other good medicyne for the same.
Take Christall,[11] and make it in fyne pouder, and myxt it wyth as moche fenell seede and sugre, and use to drynke it warme with a lytle wyne.

A playstre for the encrease of mylke.
Take fenelle and hoorehounde, of every one two handefulles, anys seede foure drammes, Saffron a scruple in poudre, swete butter thre ounces; seeth them in water, and make a playstre to be layed upon the nurces brestes.

These thynges have propertye to augment the mylke: dylle, anyse seede, fenelle, cristal, horehounde, fresh chese, honye, lettuse, beetes, myntes, carette rootes, parsneppes, the dugges or ydder of a cowe or a shepe, gootes mylke, blaunched almondes, ryce porryge, a cowes tounge dryed and made in pouder, poched egges, saffron, and the juce of rosted veale dronken.

Thus moche of the nource and of the mylke; nowe wyll I declare the infirmities of chyldren.

Althoughe (as affirmeth Plinie) there be innumerable passions and diseases whereunto the bodye of man is subjecte, and as well maye chaunce in the yonge as in the olde, yet for mooste commonlye the tender age of chyldren is chefely vexed and greved with these diseases folowynge:

Aposteme of the brayne.
Swellyng of the heed.
Scalles of the heed.
Watchyng out of measure.
Terrible dreames.
The fallyng evyll.

---

[10] i.e., ox, cow, or heifer.
[11] i.e., quartz.

The palsye.
Crampe.
Styfnesse of lymmes.
Bloodshotten eyes.
Watryng eyes
Scabbynesse and ytche.
Diseases in the eares.
Nesyng out of measure.
Bredyng of teeth.
Cankre in the mouth
Quynsye, or swellyng of throte
Coughe
Straytnesse of wynde.
Feblenesse of the stomake and vomytyng.
Yeaxyng or hycket.
Colyke and romblyng in the guttes.
Fluxe of the belly
Stoppyng of the bellye
Wormes.
Swellyng of the navyll.
The stone.
Pyssyng in bedde.
Brustynge.
Fallyng of the fundament
Chafyng of the skynne.
Small pockes and measels
Fevers.
Swellyng of the coddes
Sacer ignis or chingles.
Burnyng and scaldyng.
Kybbes.
Consumption.
Leanenesse.
Gogle eyes.

Of aposteme of the brayne.

In the filme that covereth the brayn chaunceth oftentymes apostemation and swellyng, eyther of too moche crying of the chylde, or by reason of the mylke immoderatelye hote, or excesse of heate in the blood, or of cold fleume, and is knowen by these sygnes:

If it be of hote matter, the heed of the chylde is unnaturally swollen, redde and hote in the feelynge; if it come of colde matter, it is somwhat swollen, pale and colde in the touchyng; but in bothe cases the chylde can not reste and is ever lothe to have hys heed touched, cryeth and vexeth it selfe as it were in a frenesye.

Remedye.

Make a bath of mallowes, camomylle, and lyllyes, sodden wyth a shepes heed tyll the bones fall, and with a sponge or soft cloutes[12] al to bathe the heed of the chylde in a colde aposteme wyth the brothe hote as maye be suffered; but in a hote matter, wyth the brothe luke warme, or in the coolynge, and after the bath, set on a playstre thus.

A playstre.

Take fenugreke, camomyll, wormwood, of every one an handfull, seethe them in a close vessell tyll the thyrde part be consumed, then stampe them in a mortar and styrre them; to the which ye shall put of the same brothe agayne ynough to make a playstre, with a lytle beane floure, yolkes of egges and saffron, addyng to them fresh butter or duckes grese suffycient, and applye it. In a colde matter, lette it lye a day; but in a hote cause ye must remove it every syxe houres.

Of swellyng of the heed.

Inflation, or swellynge of the heed, commeth of a wyndye matter gathered betwene the skynne and the flesh, and sometyme betwene the fleshe and the boones of the sculle, the tokens wherof are manifest ynough to the syght by the swellynge or puffing up; and pressed with the fynger, there remayneth a prynte whyche is a sygne of wynde and viscous humours; ye shall heale it thus.

Remedye.

Fyrst, let the nourse avoyde al thinges that engendre wynde, salt or slymy humours, as beanes, peason, eles, sammon, saltfyshe, and lyke; then make a playster to the chyldes heed, after this fashion:

Take an handefull of fenell, smallache and dylle, and seethe them in water in a close vessell; afterwarde stampe them, and wyth a lytle cu-

---

[12] cloths, or compresses.

myne and oyle of bytter almondes, make it uppe and laye it often to the chyldes heed, warme. In default of oyle of almons take gosegrese, addyng a litle vynegre

And it is good to bathe the place with a softe cloute or a sponge in the broth of these herbes: rue, tyme, majorym, hysope, fenelle, dylle, comyne, sal nitre, myntes, radysh rotes, rocket, or some of them, ever takynge heede that there droppe no portion of the medycynes in the babes eyes, mouthe, or eares.

Scalles of the heed.

The heedes of chyldren are oftentymes ulcered and scalled, as well when they sucke, and then mooste commonlye by reason of sharpe mylke, as also when they have bene weaned and can go aloone Sometymes it happeneth of an evyll complexion of humours by eatynge of rawe frute or other evyll meates, and sometyme by longe continuynge in the sonne, manye tymes by droppynge of restye bacon or of salte beefe on theyr bare heedes [13]

Otherwhyles, they be so borne oute of their mothers wombe; and in all these is no greate difficultie tyl the heere be growen But after that, they requyre a greater cure and a connyng hande, notwythstandynge, as God shall gyve me grace, here shal be sayde remedyes for the cure of them, suche as have ben oftentymes approved, wherein I have entended to omytte the disputations of the dyfference of scalles, and the humours whereof they do proceade, and wyll go strayght to the composition of medicynes, folowynge the good experyence here ensuynge.

Remedyes for scalles.

Yf ye see the scalles lyke the shelles of oysters, blacke and drye, cleavynge upon the skynne one within an other, ye maye make a fomentation of hoote and moyste herbes, as fenugreke, holyhocke, beares breache, lyneseede, and suche other, sodden al or some of them in the brothe of netes feete, and so to bathe the sores, and after that applye a

---

[13] On this point, Neale and Wallis (8) speculated about accidents in the home In their 1957 reprint, they report the following communication

> Mr D F Lewis, of London, has written about the dropping of the restye bacon, ... and points out that it was not the joints themselves, but drops and fragments which fell He adds that in remote parts of Wales old women still wear caps indoors to save them from baldness, which might be induced by contact with bacon and ham. It may be that ringworm was sometimes transmitted in this way (10).

softe playstre of the same herbes, and gosegrese or butter, usynge this styll tyll ye see the scabbe removed, and then wasshe it with the juce of horehounde, smallache and betony, sodden togyther in wyne; and after the wasshynge put upon it pouder of myrre, aloes and frankensence, or holde hys heed over a chafyngdysshe of coles wherin ye shall put frankensence and saunders in pouder. But if ye see the scabbes be verye sore and matrye with great payne and burnynge of the heed, ye shall make an oyntment to coole the matter thus.

An oyntment to coole the burnynge of a sore heade.

Take whyte leade and lytarge,[14] of everye one .v. drammes, lye made of the asshes of a vyne .iii. drammes, oyle of roses an ounce, waxe an ounce; melte the waxe fyrst, then putte to the oyle and lye wyth the reste, and in the ende .ii. yolkes of egges; make an oyntmente and laye it to the head. Thys is the composition of Rasis.

An other oyntment singuler for the same pourpose.

Take betonye, grounswel, plantayn, fumytorie, and daysies, of every one lyke moche; stampe them, and myngle them with a pounde of fresshe swynes grece, and lette them stande closed in a moyst place .viii. dayes to putrify; then frye them in a panne, and strayne them into a cleane vessell; and ye shall have a grene oyntmente of a singuler operation for the sayde dysease and to quenche all unkind heates of the bodye.

Also ye muste use to shave the head, whatsoever thynges ye doo laye unto it.

If there lacketh cleansyng of the sores, and the chylde weaned, ye shall do wel to make an oyntment of a lytle turpentyne, bulles gall, and hony, and lay upon the sores.

Also it is proved that the uryne of a bulle is a singuler remedy to mundifie the sores and to lose the heares by the rootes without any peyne or pille.

The juyce also of morell, daysie leaves, and groundswell, fryed wyth grece and made in an oyntmente, cooleth all unkynde heates and pustles of the heade.

Here is to be noted that, durynge thys dysease in a suckynge chylde, the nourse muste avoyde all salte and sower meates that engender chol-

---

[14] lead protoxide.

ere, as mustarde, vynegre and such, and all maner frutes (excepte a pomegranat); and she must abstayne in this case both from egges and frome other kynde of whyte meates in general; and above al she maye eate no dates, figges, nor purcelane, for manye holde opynion that purcelane hath an evylle propertye to breede scabbes and ulcers in the head. Moreover the childes head may not be kepte too hote, for that is oftentymes the cause of thys dysease.

Sometymes it chaunceth that there breadeth in the heade of chyldren as it were litle wartes or knobbes somwhat harde, and can not be resolved by the sayde medicines. Wherefore when ye see that none other thynge wyll healpe, ye shall make an good oyntmente to remove it, in maner as hereafter is declared.

An excellent remedye for wartes or knobbes of the head.

Take lytarge and whyte lead, of eche a lyke quantitie, brymstone[15] and quycksylver quenched wyth spyttle, of eche a lesse quantitie, twyse as moch oyle of roses, and a sponefull or .ii. of vynegre, mixe them all togyther on a marble til they be an oyntment, and laye it on the head; and whan it hath ben drye an houre or ii. wasshe it off with water wherein was sodden majorym, savery, and mintes, use it thus twyse a daye, mornynge and evenynge, tylle ye see it whole. This thyng is also good in all the other kind of scalles.

Of watchyng out of measure.

Slepe is the nouryshment and foode of a suckyng chylde, and as much requisyte as the very tete; wherfore whan it is depryved of the naturalle reste, all the whole bodye falleth in distemper, cruditie, and wekenes. It procedeth commonly by corruption of the milke, or too moch aboundans, whyche overladeth the stomacke, and, for lacke of good dygestion, vapoures and fumes aryse into the head and infect the brayne, by reason wherof the chyld can not slepe but turneth and vexeth it selfe with cryeng. Therfore it shall be good to provoke it to a naturall sleepe thus, accordyng to Rasis.

Annoynte the forehead and temples of the chylde wyth oyle of vyolettes and vynegre, puttynge a droppe or .ii. into the nosethrylles. And

---

[15] sulphur

yf ye can get anye syrupe of poppye, gyve it the chylde to lycke, and then make a playstre of oyle of saffron, lettuse, and the juyce of poppie, or wet cloutes in it, and lay it overthwarte the temples.

Also the seades and the heades of popie, called chessbolles, stamped wyth rosewater and myxte wyth womans mylke and the whyte of an egge beaten all togyther and made in a playster, causeth the chylde to receyve hys naturall slepe.

Also an oyntmente made of the seede of popie and the heades, one ounce, oyle of lettuse and of popie, of eche .ii. ounces; make an oyntmente and use it.

They that can not gette these oyles maye take the herbes or juyce of lettuse, purcelane, houseleke, and popie; and with womans mylke make a playster, and laye it to the foreheade.

Oyle of vyolettes, of roses, of nenuphar, are good, and oyle of populeon, the broth of mallowes sodden, and the juyce of water plantayne.

Of terryble dreames and feare in the sleape.

Oftentymes it happeneth that the chyld is afrayde in the slepe, and somtymes waketh sodaynlye and sterteth, sometyme shryketh and trembleth, whyche affecte commeth of the arysynge of stynkynge vapoures oute of the stomacke into the fantasye and sences of the brayne, as ye may perceyve by the breath of the childe wherfore it is good to gyve hym a lytle hony to swallowe, and a lytle pouder of the seedes of peony, and sometymes tryacle in a lytle quantitie wyth mylk, and to take hede that the chylde slepe not wyth a full stomake, but to beare it aboute wakynge tyll parte be dygested, and whan that it is layde, not to rocke it moche, for overmoche shakynge letteth[16] dygestion and maketh the chyld manye tymes to vomyte.

The fallynge evylle called in the Greke tonge epilepsia.

Not only other ages but also lytle chylderne are oftentymes afflicted wyth thys grevous sycknes, somtyme by nature receyved of the parentes, and then it is impossyble or dyfficile to cure, sometyme by evyl

---

[16] i.e., hinders, impedes.

and unholsome dyete, whereby there is engendred many colde and moyst humors in the brayne wherupon thys infirmitie procedeth; whych yf it be in one that is younge and tender, it is verye harde to be removed, but in them that are somewhat stronge, as of .vii. yeres and upwarde, it is more easye.

I fynde that manye thynges have a naturall vertue agaynste the fallyng evell, not of any quality elemental but by a singuler propertie, or rather an influence of heaven, whyche almyghtye God hath gyven unto thynges here in earth, as be these and other.

Saphires, smaragdes,[17] redde coral, pyonie, mystletow of the oke taken in the monethe of Marche and the moone decreasynge, tyme, savein, dylle, and the stone that is founde in the bellye of a yong swallow, beyng the fyrste broode of the dame These, or one of them, hanged about the necke of the childe saveth and preserveth it from the sayde syckenes Nowe wyl I descrybe some good and holsome medicines to be taken inward for the same dysease.

If the chylde be not very younge, the mawe of a leveret, dronke with water and honye cureth the same

A medicine for the fallinge syckenes
Take the roote of pyony· and make it into pouder, and gyve it to the chylde to lycke in a lytle pappe and suger. They that are of age maye eate of it a good quantitie at ones and lykewise of the blacke seedes of the same pyonie.

Item, the purple violettes that crepeth on the grounde in gardeynes wyth a longe stalke, and is called in Englysh hartesease, dronken in water or in water and honye, helpeth thys dysease in a young chylde.

Moreover the muscle of the oke, rased and gyven in mylke or in water and honye, is good.

Also ye maye dystylle a water of the floures of lynd; it is a tree called in Latyne tilia, the same wherof they make ropes and halters of the barke; take the same floures and dystyll a water, and lette the pacient drynke of it nowe and then a sponefull, it is a good remedye.

Item, the rote of the sea thystle called Eringium in Latyne, eaten in broth or dronken.

Some wryte that cicorie is a singuler remedye for the same dysease. It is mente by wylde cicorie, growyng in the cornes.

---

[17] emeralds

The floures of rosemarye, made in a conserva, hath the same effecte im curynge this dysease.

I coulde declare many other remedies commended of authours, but at thys tyme these shall be sufficient

Nowe I wylle entreate somewhat of the palsey

Of the palseye or shakynge of membres.

The cure of the palsey in a chyld is not lyke to that whyche is in elder age, for the synowes of a chylde be verye nesshe[18] and tender, and therfore they ought to have a moch weacker medicyne, evermore regardynge the power of the syckenes and the vertue or debilitie of the greved paciente

For some tymes the chylde can not lyfte nother legges nor armes, whiche, yf it happen durynge the suckyng, then must the nource use a dyet enclynyng to hote and drye, and to eate spyces as galingale, cinamome, gynger, macis, nutmygges, and suche other wyth rosted and fryed meates, but abstayne frome mylke and al maner fysshe And it shal be good for her to eate a lectuary made after thys sorte.

Take myntes, cynamome, cumyne, roseleaves dryed, mastyke, fenugreke, valerian, ameos doronici, zedoary, cloves, saunders, and lignum aloes, of everye one a dramme, muske halfe one dramme; make an electuarye wyth clarifyed honye, and let her eate of it, and gyve the chylde as much as halfe a nut every daye to swalowe

A playster

Take an ounce of waxe and a dramme of euphorbium at the potecaries, and temper it wyth oyle olyve on the fyer, and make a sereclothe to comforte the backe bone and the synewes.

A goodly lavatory for the same pourpose.

Take lye of asshes, and seth therein baye buries and as moch pionie seedes in a close vessel to the thyrde parte, and wasshe the chylde often with the same.

Item, a bathe of saverye, majorym, tyme, sage, nepte, smallage, and

---

[18] The *OED* defines "nesh" as "Soft in texture or consistency, yielding easily to pressure or force " It cites Phaer's use here as early instance.

myntes, or some of them, is very good and holesome.

Also to rubbe the backe of the chylde, and the lymmes, wyth oyles of roses and spyke myxte togyther warme; and in stede of it ye may take oyle of bayes.

Of the crampe or spasmus.

Thys disease is often sene among chyldren, and commethe verye lightlye, as of debilitye of the nerves and cordes or els of grosse humours that suffocate the same; the cure of the whyche is declared of authours to be done by frictions and oyntmentes that comfort the synowes and dyssolve the matter, as oyle of floure de luyce, wyth a lytle anyse, saffron, and the rootes of pyonye. Item, oyle of camomyll, fenugreke, and mellilote, or the herbes sodden, betonie, wormwood, verveyne, and tyme, are excedynge good to washe the chylde in.

Item, the playster of euphorbium, written in the cure of palsey.

Of the styfnes or starknes of lymmes.

Sometyme it hapeneth that the lymmes are starke and can not well come togyther wythoute the greater peyne, whyche thynge procedeth many tymes of colde as whan a chylde is founde in the frost or in the strete, caste awaye by a wycked mother or by some other chaunce; although I am not ignorant that it may procede of manye other causes, as it is sayde of Rasis and of Arnolde de Villa Nova in hys booke of the cure of infantes.

And here is to be noted a wounderfulle secrete of nature, manye tymes approved, wrytten of Avicenne in hys fyrste Canon, and of Celius Antiquarum electionum, libro. xiii. capit. xxxvi. that whan a membre is utterly benummed and taken thorough colde, so that the paciente can not feele hys lymmes nor moove them accordynge to nature by reason of the vehement congelation of the blood, in suche case the chyefest helpe or remedie is not to sette them to the fyer to receyve heate, for by that meanes lyghtlye we see that every one swowneth and many dye oute ryghte, but to sette the fete, legges, and armes in a payle of clere colde water, whyche immediatlye shal dissolve the congelation and restore the bloode to the former passage and fredome; after that ye may laye the pacient in a bedde to sweate, and gyve hym hote drynke and cawdels,[19] or a coleys[20] of a capon hote, wyth a lytle cynamome and saffron to comforte the harte. An argumente of this cure ye maye see thus:

When an apple or a pere is frosen in the wynter, sette it to the fyer and it is destroyed; but yf ye putte it into colde water, it shall as well endure as it dyd afore; whereby it doth appere that the water resolveth colde better wyth his moysture than the fyer can do by reason of hys heate, for the water relenteth and the fyer draweth and dryeth, as affyrmeth Galiene in hys booke of elementes.

Hytherto have I declyned by occasion, but I truste not in vayne to the reder. Nowe to my purpose.

When a yonge chylde is so taken with a colde, I esteme it best for to bathe the bodye in luke warme water wherein hath ben sodden majorym and tyme, ysope, sage, myntes, and suche other good and comfortable herbes, then to releve it wyth meates of good nouryshment accordyng to the age and necessitie, and, yf nede be, when ye see the lymmes yet to be starke, make an oyntment after this fourme.

An oyntment for styffe and stoyned lymmes.

Take a good handfull of nettle and stampe them, then seeth them in oyle to the thyrde parte in a double vessel; kepe that oyntment in a drye place, for it wyl last a great whyle and is a singuler remedye for the styfnesse that commeth of cold, and whoso anoynteth his handes and feete with it in the mornynge shall not be greved wyth colde all the daye after.

The seedes of nettles gathered in harvest and kept for the same entent is excedyng good, sodden in oyle or fryed with swynes grese; whych thyng also is very good to heale the kybbes of heeles,[21] called in Latyn Perniones.

The uryne of a goote, with the donge stamped and layed to the place, resolveth the styfnesse of lymmes.

When the cause commeth not by extreme colde but of some other affection of the synowes and cordes, it is best to make a bath or a fomentation of herbes that resolve and comfort the synowes with relaxation of the grosse humours, and to open the pores as by example thus: Take malowes, holyhocke, and dyll, of eche a handful or two, seeth

---

[19] i.e., caudles; gruels, often spiced and mixed with wine and beer.
[20] i.e., cullis; a strong meat broth.
[21] i.e., chilblains: inflammatory swelling produced by exposure to cold. A "kibe" is a chapped or ulcerated chilblain, usually occurring on the heel. The *OED* cites Phaer's use here. See Phaer's particular treatment "Of kybes" (73–74).

them in the water of netes feete, or in broth of flesh wythout salt wyth a handfull of bran and comyne, in the which ye shall bathe the chylde as warme as he may suffre; and yf ye see necessitie, make a playstre wyth the same herbes and laye it to the griefe wyth a lytle gosegrese or duckes grese or, yf it maye be gotten, oyle of camomylle, of lylyes, and of dylle. Cloutes wette in the sayde decoction, and layed about the membres, helpeth.

Of bloodshotten eyes, and other infirmities.

Somtyme the eyes are bloodshotten, and other whyles encreasyng a fylthye and whyte humoure coverynge the syght; the cause is often of too moche crying, for the which it is good to drop in the eyes a lytle of the juce of nyghtshade, otherwyse called morel, and to anoynt the forheed with the same, and yf the eye swell, to wette a cloute in the juce and the whyte of egges, and laye it to the grefe.

If the humour be clammysshe and tough and cleveth to the corners of the eyes so that the chylde can not open them after his slepe, it shall be removed with the juce of houseleeke dropped on the eye with a fether.

When the eye is bloodshotten and redde, it is a synguler remedye to put in it the bloode of a yonge pigion or a dove or a partryche, eyther hote from the byrde or els dried and made in pouder as subtyle as maye be possyble

A playstre for swellyng and payne of the eyes

Take quynces and cromes of whyte bread and seeth them in water tyl they be softe, then stampe them, and, wyth a lytle saffron and the yolkes of two egges, make a playstre to the childes eyes and foreheed. Ye maye let hym also to receyve the fume of that decoction It is also good in the meygrym. Yf ye wyl have further, loke in *The Regyment of Lyfe* in the declaration of paynes of the heed [22]

---

[22] The first chapter of Goeurot's *The Regiment of Lyfe* concerns "sycknesse and remedyes of the heed " Phaer translates the section on "meygrym" thus:

There is nothyng that is so convenient for the meygrym as tranquillitie and rest, and let al thinges pase that move the vertue animall, as great musynges and all laboure of the spyrites And chefely one ought after dynner to kepe hym from all thynges that trouble the memorye, as studyinge, readynge, wrytyng, and other lyke (A8v)

Of watrynge eyes.

If the chyldes eyes water overmoche wythout crying, by reason of a distillation commyng from the heed, Manardus teacheth a goodly playstre to restrayne the reumes, and is made thus:

Hartes horne brente to pouder and wasshed twyse, guaiacum, otherwyse called lignum sanctum, corticum thuris, antimonye, of eche one part, muske, the .iii. parte of one parte; make a fyne pouder and use it with the juce or water of fenell.

These thynges have vertue to staunche the rennyng of eyes: the shelles of snayles brent, the tycke that is found in the dugges of kyne, philipendula, frankensence and the whyte of a egge layed upon the foreheed, flewort or the water wherin it is steped, tutie,[23] the water of buddes of oke styled, beanefloure fynelye syfted, and with the gumme of a cherytree steped in vinegre and layd over al the temples.

Of scabbynesse and ytche.

Sometyme by reason of excesse of heate, or sharpenesse in the mylke throughe the nourses eatyng of salt and eygre meates, it happeneth that a chyld is sene ful of ytch by rubbing, fretyng, and chafynge of it selfe, encreaseth a scabbe called of the Grekes Psora: whyche thynge also chaunceth unto many after they be weaned, proceding of salt and adust[24] humoures; the cure whereof dyffereth in none other but accordyng to the difference of age, for in a suckyng babe the medicines may not be so sharpe as it maye be suffered in one that is all readye weaned. Agaynste suche unkynde ytche, ye maye make an oyntment thus.

Take water betony, .ii. good handfulles, daysye leaves and alehofe otherwyse called tumnour or grounde yvye, of eche one handfull, the red docke rootes, two or thre; stampe them all togyther and grynde them well, then myngle them wyth fresshe grese and agayne stampe them. Lette them so stande .viii. dayes to putrifye tyll it be hore, then frye them out and strayne them and kepe it for the same entent.

This oyntment hath a greate effecte both in yonge and olde, and that wythout repercussion or dryving backe of the matter whyche shoulde be a peryllouse thynge in a yonge chylde.

---

[23] zinc oxide.
[24] inordinately dry.

The herbe water betonye alone is a great medicyne to quenche all unkynde heates without daunger, or the sethyng of it in cleare welle water to annoynte the membres. It is a comon herbe, and groweth by ryvers sydes and smal rennyng waters and wette places, arysing many tymes the heygth of a man out of the grounde, where he rejoyseth wyth a stalke foure square and many braunches on every syde; and also it beareth a whytysh blewe flowre very small, and in harvest it hath innumerable seedes, blacke and as fyne as the seede of tutsone or lesse; the leves bygge and long accordyng to the grounde, full of juyce, jagged on the sydes lyke a sawe even as other betonye to whome it approcheth in figure, and obteineth his name of water betonye. The savoure of the leafe is somewhat heavye, mooste lyke to the savour of elders or walwort, but when it is brused it is more pleasaunt; whyche thyng induceth me to vary from the myndes of them that thynke thys herbe to be Galiopsis in Dioscorides, wrytten of hym that it shoulde stynke when it is stamped. But the more thys herbe is stamped, the more swete and herbelyke it savoureth Therfore it can not be galiopsis; and besydes that, it is never founde in drye and stony grounde as the Galiopsis is. Neyther is thys herbe mencyoned of the newe or olde authours, as farre as I can see, but of onely Vigo, the famous surgyon of our tyme in Italye, whyche wryteth on it that thys herbe exceadeth all other in a malo mortuo (so calleth he a kynde of leprye elephantyk or an universal and fylthye scabbe of all the bodye), and in lyke maner, he sayeth it is good for to cure a canker in the breastes Ye maye reade these thynges in his second boke, Capitul .iii , and hys fyfth booke of the Frenche pockes, in the thyrde chapiter, where he doth descrybe thys aforesayd herbe wyth so manyfeste tokens that no man wyll doubt it to be water betonye, conferryng the boke and the herbe duly togyther. Moreover he nameth in Italye a brydge where it groweth in the water in greate aboundaunce, and called of that nacyon Alabeveratore, whych indede the Italyons that come hyther, and knowe bothe the place and the herbe, do affyrme playnely it is our water betonye.

And whereas he allegeth Dioscorides in clymeno, whych by contemplation of both hath but small affinitie or none wyth thys herbe, it was for nothynge els but lacke of the tonges, which faulte is not to be so hyghly rebuked in a man of his studye, applyinge hymselfe more to the practyse of surgerye and to handye operation, wherein indede he was nere incomparable, than he dyd to search the varyaunce of tonges, and rather regarded to declare the operation of thynges wyth truthe than to despute upon the propertyes of names with eloquence.

Thus have I declyned agayne from my matter, partly to shewe the descryption of this holesome herbe, partely to satysfye the myndes of the surgions in Vigo, whyche have hytherto redde the sayde places in vayne, and furthermore bycause there is yet none that declareth manifestly the same herbe.

*An other remedye for scabbes
and ytche.*

Take the rootes of dockes and frye them in fresh grese, then put to it a quantitye of brymstone in pouder and use to rubbe the places twyse or thryse a day. Brimstone poudred and souped in a rere egge healeth the scabbes, whych thyng is also very good to destroye wormes.

*A goddly swete sope for scabbes
and ytche.*

Take whyte sope halfe a pounde and stepe it in suffycient rosewater tyl it be well soked; then take two drammes of mercurye sublymed, dissolve it in a lytle rosewater, labour the sope and the rosewater wel together, and afterward put in it a lytle muske or cyvette[25] and kepe it. This sope is excedynge good to cure a greate scabbe or ytche, and that wythoute peryll, but in a chylde it shall suffyce to make it weaker of the mercurye.

*An other approved medicyne for
scabbynesse and ytche.*

Take fumyterrie, docke rootes, scabiouse, and the roote of walwort, stampe them all and set them in freshe grese to putrifye; then frye them and strayne them, in whych lycour ye shal put turpentine a lytle quantitie, brymstone and frankensence very fynely poudred and syfted a portion; and with suffycient waxe make an oyntment on a softe fyre. Thys is a synguler remedy for the same purpose. But in thys cure ye ought to gyve the chylde no egges nor anye eygre or sharpe meat; and the nurse also must avoyde the same, and not to wrappe it in too hoote, and yf neade be, to make a bath of fumyterrye, centaurye, fetherfewe, tansye, wormewood, and sauce, alone yf ye see the cause of the ytche or the scabbe to be wormes in the skynne, for a bytter decoction shal destroy them and drye up the moystures of the sores.

---

[25] i.e., civet; musky perfuming substance obtained from anal glands of the civet cat (*Civettica civetta*) of central Africa.

Of diseases in the eares.

Many dyseases happen in the eares, as payne, apostemes, swellynges, tynclyng and sound in the heed, stoppyng of the organes of hearynge, water, wormes, and other infortunes gotten into the eares; wherof some of them are daungerous and harde to be cured, some other expelled of nature without medicyne.

Remedye for payne in the eares.

For payne in the eares withoute a manifest cause, as often chaunceth, it is a singuler remedye to take the chest wormes that are founde under barkes of trees or in other stompes in the ground, and wyll tourne rounde lyke a pease. Take of them a good quantytye and seeth them in oyle in the rynde of a pomegranade on the hote ymbres that it brenne not, and after that strayne it and put into the eares a droppe or two luke warme, and then lette hym lye upon the other eare and reste. Ye maye gyve thys to all ages, but in a chylde ye must put a very lytle quantitie

An other.

The hame or skynne of an adder or a snake that she casteth, boyled in oyle and dropped into the eares, easeth the payne, and it is also good for an eare that mattereth,[26] myngled with a lytle honye and put in luke warme. It is also good to droppe into the eares the juyce of organye and mylke.

For swellyng under the eares.

Paynters oyle, whych is oyle of lyne seed, is excedyng good for the swellyng of the eares and for payne in the eares of all causes.

Item, a playstre made of lyneseede and dylle with a lytle duckes grese and honye

Yf ye see the aposteme breake and renne, ye maye clense it with the juce of smallach, the whyte of an egge, barly floure and honye, which is a comon playstre to mundifye a sore.

When the eares have receyved water or any other licour, it is good to take and stampe an onyon and wryng out the juce with a lytle gosegrese, and droppe it hote into the eare as it may be suffred and laye hym downe on the contrarye syde an houre. After that, cause hym to

---

[26] i e , to discharge matter; to suppurate The *OED* cites Phaer's use

nese,[27] yf hys age wyll suffre, wyth a lytle pellitorie of Spayne or nesyng pouder, and then enclyne hys eare downewarde that the water maye yssue.

For wormes in the eares.

Take myrre, aloes, and the seede of colocynthis, called coloquintida of the apothecaries, a quantitie of eche, seethe them in oyle of roses and put a lytle in the ears.

Myrre hath a great vertue to remove the stynche that is caused in the eares by any putrefaction; and the better wyth oyle of bytter almondes, or ye may take the juce of wormewood wyth hony and salt peter

For wynde in the eares and tynklynge.

Take myrre, spykenarde, cummyne, dylle, and oyle of camomylle, and put a droppe in the eares. They that have not all these maye take some of them and applye it accordyng to discretion.

To amende deafnesse, ye shall make an oyntment of an hares galle and the grese or droppyng of an ele, which is a soverayne thyng to recover hearyng.

Of nesyng out of measure.

When a chylde neseth oute of measure, that is to saye with a longe continuance and therby the brayne and vertues animall be infebled, it is good to stoppe it to avoyde a further inconvenyence

Wherfore ye shall annoynt the heade wyth the juyce of purcelane, sorell, and nyghtshade, or some of them; and make a playster of the whyte of an egge and the juyce, wyth a lytle oyle of roses, and emplayster the forheade and temples wyth the mylke of a woman, oyle of roses, and vynegre a lytle

If it come of a colde reume, ye shall make a playster of mastyke, frankynsens, myrre, wyne, and applye it to the former parte of the head. A fume of the same receyved in flaxe, and layed upon the chyldes head, is holsome.

---

[27] sneeze.

Breedynge of teeth.

About the seventh moneth, somtyme more, sometyme lesse, after the byrthe, it is natural for a chylde for to breede teeth; in which time many one is sore vexed wyth sondrye dyseases and peynes, as swellynge of the gummes and jawes, unquyete cryenge, fevers, crampes, palsies, fluxes, reumes, and other infyrmities, speciallye whan it is longe or the teeth come fourth, for the soner they apere, the better and more ease it is to the chylde.

There be dyvers thynges that are good to procure an easy breedyng of teeth, among whom the chyefest is to annoynt the gummes wyth the braynes of an hare myxte wyth as much capons grece and honye; or anye of these thynges alone is exceadynge good to supple the gummes and the synewes

Also it is good to wasshe the chylde two or three tymes in a weeke wyth warme water or the decoction of camomyll, hollyhocke, and dylle

Fresshe butter wyth a lyttle barlye floure, or honye wyth the fyne pouder of frankynsence and liquirice, are commended of good authours for the same entent.

And whan the peyne is greatte and intollerable wyth aposteme or inflammation of the gommes, it is good to make an oyntmente of oyle of roses with the juyce of morelle, otherwyse called nyghtshade, and in lacke of it, annoynt the jawes wythin wyth a lytle fresshe butter and honye.

For lacke of the hares brayne ye may take the conyes, for they be also of the kynde of hares, and called of Plinye Dasypodes, whose mawes are of the same affecte in medicyne or rather more than is wrytten of authoures of the mawes of hares.

If ye see the gommes of the chyld to aposteme or swelle wyth softe flesshe full of matter and paynefulle, the beste shall be to annoynt the sore place wyth the brayne of an hare and capons grece, equallye myxt togyther; and after that ye have used thys ones or twyse, annoynte the gommes and apostemations wyth honye.

Thyrdlye, yf thys helpe not, take turpentyne myxte wyth a lytle honye in equal portion, and make a bathe for the head of the chylde in thys fourme:

Take the floures of camomyll and dyll, of eche an handeful, seeth them in a quarte of pure rennynge water untyl they be tender, and wasshe the head afore anye meate every mornynge, for it pourgeth the superfluytye of the braynes thorough the seames of the skull, and wythdraweth humours frome the sore place, fynally comforteth the brayne and all the vertues anymall of the chyld.

To cause an easie breedyng of teeth, many thinges are rehersed of auctours besydes the premisses: as the fyrste cast teeth of a colte, set in sylver and borne; or redde coralle in lyke maner, hanged about the necke wheruppon the chylde shulde oftentymes labour his gummes; and many other lyke, whyche I leave out at thys tyme to avoyde tediousnes, onely content to declare thys of corall: that by consent of all authours it resisteth the force of lyghtenynge, helpeth the chyldren of the fallynge evyll, and is very good to be made in pouder and dronken agaynst all maner of bleedyng of the nose or fundament.

Of a canker in the mouthe.

Manytymes by reson of corruption of the mylke, venymous vapoures arysynge from the stomake, and of many other infortunes, there chaunceth to brede a canker in the mouthes of chyldren, whose sygnes are manifeste ynough, that is to say by stinkynge of the mouthe, peyne in the place, contynuall rennynge of spyttle, swelling of the cheke; and when the mouth is opened agaynst the sonne, ye maye see clerelye where the canker lyeth. It is so named of the latter sorte of phisitions by reason of crepynge and eatynge forwarde and backewarde and spreadeth it selfe abrode lyke the feete of a crevis,[28] called in Latyne cancer. Notwithstandynge, I knowe that the Greekes and aunciente Latynes gyve other names unto this dysease, as in callynge it an ulcer, other whyles aphthe, nome, carcinoma, and lyke, whiche are al in Englyshe knowen by the name of canker in the mouthe. And although there be many kyndes accordyng to the matter wherof they be engendred, and therfore requyre a dyversitie of curyng, yet for the most parte whan they be in chylderne the cure of them all differeth verye lytle or nothyng. For the chyefe entent shall be to remove the malignitye of the sore and to drye up the noysome matter and humours, then to mundify and heale as in other kyndes of ulcers, sores, and woundes.

Remedies for the canker in the mouthe of chyldren.

Take drye redde roses and violettes, of eche a lyke quantity, make them in pouder and myxte them wyth a lytle honye; thys medycyne is verye

---

[28] crayfish or crab.

good in a tender suckynge chylde, and many tymes healeth alone wythout any other thyng at all.

But yf ye see there be greate heate and burnynge in the sore with excedyng payne, ye shall make a juyce of purselane, lettuse, and nyghteshade, and wasshe the sore wyth a fyne pece of sylke or dryve it in wyth a spoute called of the surgions a syrynge.

Thys, by the grace of God, shall abate the brennynge, aswage the peyne, and kyll the venyme of the ulcer.

But yf ye see the canker yet encrease wyth greate corruption and matter, ye shall make an oyntment after this maner:

Take myrre, galles wherewyth they make ynke, or in defaulte of them oken apples dryed, frankynsence, of eche a lyke moche, of the blacke bureis growynge on the bramble taken frome the busshe whyle they be grene, the thyrde parte of all the reste; make them all in pouder, and myxte them wyth as moch honye and saffron as is sufficient, and use it.

A stronger medicine for the canker in the mouth of chyldren

Take the roote of celidonie dryed, the rynde of a pomegranate, redde corall in pouder, and the pouder of a hartes horne, of eche a lyke, roche alume[29] a lytle, fyrste wasshe the place wyth wyne, or warme water and honye, and afterwarde putte on the foresayd pouder very fyne and subtile.

An other singuler medecyne for the canker in the mouthe of all ages.

Rx. ysope, sage, rue, of eche one good handefull; sethe them in wyne and water to the thyrde part, then strayne them out and putte in it a lytle whyte coperose[30] accordynge to necessytye; that is to saye, whan the sore is greatte putte in the more, whan it is smalle ye maye take the lesse; then adde to it a quantitie of honye clarifyed and a sponefull or .ii of good aqua vite; washe the place wyth it, for it is a synguler remedy to remoove the malyce in a shorte whyle, whyche done, ye shall make a water incarnatyve and healynge thus:

Rx. rybworte, betonye, and daysies, of eche a handefull, seethe them

---

[29] rock alum
[30] zinc protosulphate.

in wyne and water, and wasshe hys mouthe .ii. or .iii. tymes a day wyth the same juce.

Moreover, some wryte that cristal made in fyne pouder hath a singuler vertue to destroye the canker; and in lyke maner the pouder of an hartes horne brent wyth as moche of the rynde of a pomegranade and the juyce of nyghtshade is very good and holsome.

Of quinsye and swellynge of the throte.

The quinsye is a daungerous syckenes bothe in yonge and olde, called in Latyne angina. It is an inflammation of the necke with swellyng and great peyne. Somtyme it lyeth in the verye throte upon the wesant pipe, and then it is excedyng perillous for it stoppeth the breath and stranguleth the pacient anone. Otherwhyles it breaketh out lyke a bonche on the one syde of the necke, and then also with verye great difficultie of breathyng; but it choketh not so sone as the fyrste doeth, and it is more obedient to receyve curation. The signes are apparaunt to syght, and besydes that the chylde can not crye, nether swallowe downe hys meat and drynke wythout payne.

Remedye.

It is good to annoynt the grefe with oyle of dylle or oyle of camomyll and lylies, and to laye upon the heade hote cloutes dipte in the waters of rosemary, lavender, and savery.

The chyefeste remedye commended of authours in thys outragious syckenes is the pouder of a swallowe brent wyth fethers and all and myxte wyth honye, whereof the pacient must swallowe downe a lytle, and the rest anoynted upon the payne. They prayse also the pouder of the chyldes dunge to the chyld, and of a man to a man, brent in a potte and anoynted wyth a lytle honye. Somme make a compounded oyntment of bothe; the receyte is thus: Rx. of the swallowe brent, one portion; of the second poudre, another; make it in a thycke fourme with honye, and it wyll endure longe for the same entent.

Item, an other experimente for the quinsy and swellynge under the eares:

Take the musherim that groweth upon an elder tree, called in Englysshe Jewes eares (for it is indede croncled and flat, moch lyke an eare), heate it agaynst the fyer and put it hote in any drynke; the same drynke is good and holsome for the quynsy.

Some holde opinion that who so useth to drynke wyth it shall never be troubled wyth this dysease, and therefore carye it about wyth them in jorneys.

Of the cough.

The cough in chyldren for the moste parte procedeth eyther of a colde or by reason of rewmes descendynge from the head into the pypes of the longes or the breast, and that is moste commonlye by overmoche aboundaunce of mylke corruptynge the stomake and brayne, therfore, in that case it is good to feede the child wyth a more slendre dyete and to annoynt the heade over wyth honye, and nowe and then to presse his tonge with your fynger, holdynge downe his head that the reumes maye issue, for by that meanes the cause of the cough shall ren out of hys mouth and avoyde the chylde of many noughtie and slymy humours; whyche done, many tymes the paciente amendeth wythout any further helpe of medicine.

For the cough in a chylde

Take gomme Arabik, gumme dragagant,[31] quynce seedes, liquyrice, and penidies,[32] at the pothecaries; breake them altogyther and gyve the chylde to suppe a lytle at ones, wyth a draught of milk newely warme as it commeth from the cowe.

Also, stampe blaunched almons and wrynge them out wyth the juyce of fenell, or water of fenell, and gyve it to the chylde to feade wyth a lytle suger

Agaynste the great cough and heate in the bodye.

The heades of whyte poppye and gumme dragagant, of eche a lyke moch, longe cucumer seades, as moche as all; seth them in whaye wyth raysons and suger, and lette the chylde drynke of it twyse or thryes a daye, luke warme or colde.

---

[31] i.e., tragacanth
[32] i.e., a stick of barley sugar

Of straytenes of wynde.

Agaynste the straytenes of brethyng whiche is no quinsie, the consent of authours do attribute a greate effecte to lyneseede made in poudre and tempered with hony for the chylde to swallowe downe a lytle at ones. I fynde also that the milke of a mare, newlye receyved of the child wyth suger, is a synguler remedye for the same pourpose.

Whyche thynge, moreover, is exceding holsome to make the bellye laxe wythout trouble.

Of weaknes of the stomacke and vomytynge.

Many tymes the stomacke of the chyld is so feble that it cannot retayne eyther meate or drynke, in which case, and for all debilitye thereof, it is very good to wasshe the stomake wyth warme water of roses wherin a lytle muske hath bene dyssolved, for that by the odour and natural heate gyveth a comforte to al the spirituall membres.

And then it is good to roste a quynce tender, and wyth a lyttle pouder of cloves and suger to gyve it to the chylde to eate; conserva quynces wyth a lyttle cynamome and cloves is singuler good for the same entent. Also ye may make a juyce of quynces, and gyve it to the child to drynke wyth a lytle suger.

An oyntment for the stomacke.

Take gallia muscata[33] at the pothecaryes, .xx. grayne weyght, myrre a very lytle; make it up in oyntmente fourme wyth oyle of mastyke and water of roses sufficient; thys is a very good oyntment for the stomacke.

An other singuler receyte.

Take mastyk, frankinsence, and drye redde roses, as moche as is sufficiente; make them in pouder, and temper them up wyth the juyce of myntes and a sponefull of vynegre, and use it.

An other.

Take wheate floure and parche it on a panne tylle it begynne to brenne and waxe redde, then stampe it wyth vynegre and adde to it the yolkes

---

[33] a medicament composed of musk, amber, and lignum aloes.

of .ii egges harde rosted, mastyke, gumme, and frankensence sufficient; make a plaistre and laye it to the stomake

To recover an appetyte lost.

Take a good handfull of ranke and lustye rewe and seeth it in a pynt of vinegre to the thyrde parte or lesse, and make it very stronge; wherof yf it be a chylde, ye maye take a tooste of browne bread, and stamp it with the same vynegre, and laye it playstrewyse to the stomake, and for a stronger age, besydes the playstre, lette hym suppe mornynge and evenyng of the same vynegre.

This is also good to recover a stomake lost by comynge to a fyre after a longe journey; and hath also a synguler vertue to restore a man that swowneth.

An experiment often approved of Rasis for the vomyte of chyldren.

Rasis, a solemne practicioner among phisicions, affirmeth that he healed a greate multitude of this dysease onelye wyth the practyse folowynge, which he taketh to be of great effecte in all lyke cases.

Fyrst he maketh as it were an electuarye of pothecarye stuffe, that is to saye, lignum aloes, mastyke, of everye one halfe a dramme, galles halfe a scruple; make a lectuarye wyth syrupe of roses and gallia muscata and sugre.

Of thys he gave the chyldren to eate a very lytle at ones and often. Afterward he made a playstre thus: Rx. mastyke, aloes, sloes, galles, frankensence, and brent bread, of eche a like portion; make a plaistre with oyle and syrupe of roses to be layed to the childes stomake hote.

An other oyntment for the stomake, descrybed of Wilhel Placentino.

Take oyle of mastyke or of wormewood ii. ounces, waxe thre ounces, cloves, maces, and cynamome, of eche thre drammes; make an oyntment, addynge in the ende a lytle vynegre

The yolke of an egge harde rosted, mastyke, frankensence, and gumme, made in a plaistre with oyle of quinces, is excedyng good for the same purpose.

Of yeaxyng or hycket.

It chaunceth oftentymes that a chylde yeaxeth out of measure. Wherfore it is expedyent to make the stomake eygre afore it be fedde, and not to replenyshe it wyth too moche at ones, for this disease commonly procedeth of fulnesse; for yf it come of emptinesse or of sharpe humours in the mouth of the stomake, which is seldom sene, the cure is then very diffycyl and daungerous.

Remedye

When it commeth of fulnesse that a chyld yeaxeth incessauntlye without measure, and that by a long custome, it is good to make him vomyt with a fether, or by some other light meanes, that the matter which causeth the yeaxynge maye yssue and uncombre the stomake That done, bryng it aslepe and use to annoynt the stomak wyth oyles of castor, spyke, camomyll, and dyll, or two or thre of them joyned togyther warme.

Of colycke and rumblynge in the guttes.

Payne in the belly is a common dysease of chyldren; it commeth eyther of woormes or of takynge colde or of evylle mylke. The sygnes thereof are too well knowen, for the chylde can not rest but cryeth and fretteth it self, and manye tymes can not make theyr uryne, by reason of wynde that oppresseth the necke of the bladder; and is knowen also by the membre in a man child whyche in this case is alwaye styffe and pryckynge, moreover, the noyse and romblyng in the guttes, hyther and thither, declareth the chylde to be greved with wynde in the bellye and colik.

Cure.

The nourse must avoyde all maner meates that engendre winde, as beanes, peason, butter, harde egges, and suche. Then wasshe the chyldes bellye wyth hote water, wherin hath ben sodden comyne, dylle, and fenell; after that, make a playstre of oyle and waxe, and clappe it hote upon a cloth unto the bellye.

An other good playstre for the same entent.

Take good stale ale and fresh butter, seeth them with an handfull of comyne poudred, and after put it all togyther into a swynes bladder, and bynde the mouthe faste that the lycoure yssue not out; then wynde it in a cloth and turne it up and downe upon the belly as hote as the pacient maye suffer. This is good for the colyke after a sodayne colde in all ages, but in chyldren ye must beware ye applye it not too hote.

Of fluxe of the bellye.

Many tymes it happeneth, eyther by takyng colde or by reson of great payne in breedynge of teethe, or els through salt and eygre fleume, or cholere engendred in the bodye, that the chylde falleth into a sodayne laxe; which yf it longe continue and be not holpen, it may brynge the pacient to extreme leanesse and consumption. Wherfore it shall be good to seke some holsome remedy and to stoppe the rennyng of the fluxe thus.

Remedye for the fluxe
in a chylde.

Fyrst make a bath of herbes that do restrayne, as of plantayne, Saint Johns weede called ypericon, knotgrasse, bursa pastoris, and other suche, or some of them, and use to bath him in it as hote as he may wel suffre, then wrappe him in with clothes, and laye him downe to slepe.

And yf ye see by this, twyse or thryse usynge, that the bellye be not stopped, ye maye take an egges yolke harde rosted, and grynde it with a lytle saffron, myrre, and wyne; make a playstre and applye it to the navyl hote. Yf this succede not, then it shal be necessarye for to make a poudre to gyve him in his meate with a litle sugre and in a smal quantitie thus·

Take the poudre of hartes horne brent, the poudre of gootes clawes or of swynes clawes brent, the poudre of the seede of roses whyche remayne in the berye when the rose is fallen, of everye one a portion; make them very fine and, with good redde wyne or almon mylke, and wheate floure, make it as it were a paste, and drye it in lytle balles tyll ye see necessitie; [it] is a singuler remedy in al suche cases.

Item, the mylke wherin hath bene sodden whyte paper, and afterwarde quenched manye hote yrons or gaddes of stele, is excedynge good for the same entent to drynke.

And here is to be noted that a natural fluxe is never to be feared afore the .vii. day; and, except there issue blood, it ought not to be stopped afore the sayde tyme.

Pouder of the herbe called knotgrasse, or the juce therof in a posset dronken, or a playstre of the same herbe and of bursa pastoris, bolearmenye,[34] and the juce of plantayne wıth a lytle vynegre and wheate floure, ıs exceadynge good for the same cause.

Also, the ryndle mawe of a yonge suckynge kydde gyven to the chylde, the weight of .x. graynes, wıth the yolke of an egge softe rosted; and let the pacyent abstayne from mylke by the space of .ıı. houres before and after, ınstede wherof ye may gyve a rosted quınce or a warden[35] wyth a lytle sugre and cynamome to eate.

Item, an other goodly receyte for the same entent.

Take sorel seed and the kernelles of greate raysyns dryed, ackorne cuppes, and the seed of whyte popye, of eche ii. drammes, saffron a good quantıtıe; make them ın pouder and tempre them wyth the juce of quynces or syrupe of red roses. Thıs ıs a soverayne thyng in al fluxes of the woumbe.

Many other thynges are wrıtten of authours in the sayd dısease, whıche I here leave out for brevıtıe and also bycause the afore reherced medicynes are suffycient ynough in a case curable. Yet wyll I not omytte a godly practyse ın the sayde cure The pesyll of an hart or a stagge, dryed in pouder and dronken, is of great and wonderful effect in stoppyng a fluxe. Whıche thyng also ıs approved in the lyver of a beaste called ın Englysshe an otter. The stones of hym, dronken ın pouder a lytle at ones, thyrtye dayes togyther, hath healed men for ever of the fallyng evyll.

Of stoppynge of the bellye.

Even as a fluxe is daungerous so is stoppynge and hardenesse of the bellye grevous and noysome to the chylde, and ıs often cause of the colycke and other diseases Wherfore in this case ye muste alwaye put a lytle hony ınto the chyldes meate, and lette the nource gyve hym honye to sucke upon her fynger; and yf this wyl not helpe, then the nexte is to myxte a lytle fyne and cleare turpentyne wyth honye, and so to resolve it in a saucer, and let the chylde suppe of ıt a lytle.

Thıs medıcine ıs descrybed of Paulus Aegıneta and recyted of dyvers other as a thyng very holsome and agreınge to the nature of the chylde,

---

[34] i e , Bole Armonıac, a varıety of frıable earthy clay, consıstıng of hydrous sılıcates of alumınum

[35] warden pear, an ancıent varıety of pear especıally favored for cooking

for it doeth not only losen the belly without grefe or daunger, but doth also purge the lyver and the longes, with the splene and kidneyes, generally comforteth all the spirituall membres of the bodye.

The gall of an oxe or a cowe, layed upon a cloute on the navylle, causeth a chylde to be loose bellyed, lykewyse an emplaystre of a rosted onyon, the galle of an oxe, and butter, layed upon the belye as hote as he maye suffre Yf these wyll not helpe, ye shal take a lytle cotten, and rolle it, and, dypped in the sayd gall, put it in the fundament.

Of wormes.

There be dyverse kyndes of wormes in the bellye, as longe, shorte, rounde, flat, and some smalle as lyce. They be all engendred of a crude, grosse, or phlegmatyke matter, and never of choler nor of melancholy, for all bytter thynges kylleth them, and al swete meates that engendre fleume nouryssheth and fedeth the same. The signes dyffer accordyng to the wormes For in the long and round, the pacient commonly hath a drye cough, payne in the belly about the guttes, some tyme yeaxynge and tremblyng in the night, and starte sodaynely and fall aslepe agayne, otherwhyles they gnasshe and grynde theyr teeth togyther, the eyes waxe holowe with an eygre loke, and have greate delyte in slombryng and sylence, verye loth when they are awaked The pulse is incertayne and never at one staye, sometyme a fever with greate colde in the joyntes, which endureth thre or .iiii. houres in the nyght or daye. Many have but small desyre to meate, and when they desyre they eate verye greedelye, whych yf they lacke at theyr appetyte they forsake it a great whyle after. The whole body consumeth and waxeth leane, the face pale or blewe; somtyme a fluxe, somtymes vomyte; and in some the belye is swollen as styffe as a taberet.

The longe and brode wormes are knowen by these sygnes, that is to saye, by yelownesse or whyttishnesse of the eyes, intollerable hungre, greate gnawynge and grypyng in the bellye, specyally afore meate, water commyng oute at the mouth or at the fundament, continuall ytche and rubbyng of the nosethrylles, sonken eyes, and a stynkyng breath; also, when the person doth his easement there appeareth in the donge lytle flat substaunces, moche like the seedes of cucumers or gourdes.

The other lesse sorte are engendred in the great gutte, and may wel be knowen by the excedynge ytche in the fundament within, and are oftentymes sene commyng out with the excrementes. They be called of phisicions ascarides.

Remedy for wormes in chyldren.

The herbe that is founde growyng upon oysters by the sees syde is a synguler remedy to destroye wormes, and is called therfore of the Grekes Scolitabotani, that is to saye, the herbe that kylleth wormes. It must be made in pouder and gyven with sweate mylke to the chylde to drynke. The phisicions call the same herbe coralina.

A singuler receyte for to
kyll wormes.

Take the gall of a bull or oxe newlye kylled, and stampe in it an handfull of good comyne; make a playstre of it and lay it over all the bellye, removyng the same every syxe houres.

Item, the galle of a bulle wyth seedes of colocynthis, called colloquintida of the pothecaryes, and an handfulle of baye beryes well made togyther in a playstre, with a sponefull of strong vynegre, is of greate effecte in the same case.

Yf the chylde be of age or stronge complexion, ye may make a fewe pilles of aloes and the pouder of wormeseed, then wynde them in a pece of singyng lofe,[36] and annoynt them over wyth a lytle butter, and lette them be swalowed downe whole without chewyng.

Of swellyng of the navyll.

In a chylde lately borne and tender, somtyme by cutting of the navyll too nere or at an inconvenient season, somtyme by swadlyng or byndynge amysse or of moche cryinge or coughynge, it happeneth otherwhyles that the navyll aryseth and swelleth wyth greate payne and apostemation; the remedy wherof is not moche differente from the cure of ulcers, savynge in thys, that ye ought to applye thynges of lesse attraction than in other kynde of ulcers; as for an example ye maye make an oyntment under thys fourme: Take spyke or lavender, halfe an ounce, make it in pouder, and wyth thre ounces of fyne and cleare turpentyne tempre it in an oyntment, addyng a portion of oyle of swete almons. But yf it come of cryinge, take a lytle beane floure and the asshes of fyne lynnen cloutes brent, and tempre it with redde wyne and honye, and laye it to the sore.

---

[36] i.e., a lump of toasted bread.

*A playstre for swellyng
in the navyll.*

Take cowes donge, and drye it in poudre, barlye floure and beane floure, of eche a porcyon, the juyce of knotgrasse a good quantitie, comyne a lytle; make a playstre of all and set it to the navyll

An other.

Take cowes donge and seeth it in the mylke of the same cowe, and laye it on the grefe. This is also marveylouse effectuall to helpe a soddayne ache or swellyng in the legges.

Of the stone in chyldren.

The tender age of children, as I sayd afore, is vexed and afflycted with manye grevous and peryllous diseases, amonge whome there is few or none so vyolent or more to be feared in them than that whyche is mooste feared in all kynde of ages, that is to saye, the stone, an houge and a pityful disease, ever the more encreasyng in dayes, the more rebellyng to the cure of Physycke.

Therfore is it excedyng daungerouse whan it falleth in chyldren. For as moch as neyther the bodyes of them may be well purged of the matter antecedent called humor peccans, nor yet can abide any vyolent medecyne havynge power to breake it, by reason wherof the sayd dysease acquyreth suche a strengthe above nature, that in processe of tyme it is utterlye incurable.

Yet in the begynnyng it is oftentymes healed thus:

Fyrste lette the nurse be wel dyeted, or the chylde yf it be of age, abstaynyng from all grosse meates and harde of digestion, as is beafe, bacon, saltemeates, and cheese; then make a pouder of the roote of peonye dryed, and myngle it wyth as moche honye as shal be sufficient; or yf the childe abhorre hony, make it up wyth suger, molten a lytle uppon the coales, and gyve thereof unto the chylde, more or lesse accordynge to the strengthe, twyse a daye tylle ye see the uryne passe easelye. Ye maye also gyve it in a rere egge, for wythout dout it is a synguler remedye in chyldren.

An oyntment for the same.

Oyle of scorpions, yf it may be gotten, is excedyng good to annoynt wythall the membres and the nether parte of the bellye ryghte agaynste the bladder; ye may have it at the pothecaries.

A singuler bathe for the same entent.

Take mallowes, holyhock, lylie rotes, lynseed, and parietarye of the wal; seeth them all in the brothe of a shepes head, and therein use to bathe the chyld oftentymes; for it shal open the straytnes of the condytes, that the stone may issue, swage the payne, and brynge oute the gravell with the uryne; but in more effecte whan a playster is made, as shal be sayde herafter, and layed uppon the raynes and the bellye immediatly after the bathynge.

A playster for the stone.

Take parietarie of the wall, one portion, and stampe it, doves dounge an other portion, and grynde it, then frye them bothe in a panne wyth a good quantitye of fresshe buttyre; and, as hote as may be suffered, laye it to the belly and the backe; and from .iii. houres to .iiii. let it be renewed.

Thys is a soverayne medicine in all maner ages.

Item, an other pouder whyche is made thus:

Take the kernels or stones that are founde in the fruyte called openers or mespiles or, of some, meddlars.[37] Make them in fyne pouder, whyche is wounderfull good for to breake the stone wythout daunger bothe in yong and olde.

The chestwoormes,[38] dryed and made in fyne pouder, taken wyth the brothe of a chycken, or a lytle suger, helpeth them that can not make theyr uryne.

Of pyssynge in the bedde.

Manytimes for debilitye of vertue retentive of the reynes or blader as wel olde men as children are oftentymes annoyed whan their urin issueth out, either in theyr sleepe or wakyng agaynst theyr wylles, havyng no power to retayne it whan it commeth. Therfore yf they wyll be holpen, fyrste they muste avoyde all fat meates tylle the vertue retentive be restored agayne, and to use thys pouder in theyr meates and drynkes:

Take the wesande of a cocke and plucke it, then brenne it in pouder

---

[37] fruit of the medlar tree, resembling a large brown apple.
[38] i.e., woodlice.

and use of it twise or thryes a daye. The stones of an hedgehogge poudred is of the same vertue.

Item, the clawes of a goate made in pouder, dronken or eaten in pottage.

If the paciente be of age, it is good to make fyne plates of leade wyth holes in them, and lette them lye often to the naked backe.

Of brustynge.

The causes of it in a chylde are many, for it maye come of very lyghte occasions, as of great cryeng and stoppynge the breath, byndynge too strayte, or by a falle; or of too greate rockynge and suche lyke maye cause the filme that spreadeth over the bellye to breake or to slacke, and so the guttes fall downe into the cod, whych yf it be not utterly uncurable maye be healed after thys sorte:

Fyrste, laye the pacient so uppon hys backe that hys heade maye be lower than hys heales, then take and reduce the bowels wyth youre hande into the due place. Afterwarde, ye shall make a playster to be layde uppon the coddes, and bounde wyth a lace rounde aboute the backe, after thys fourme

Take rosyn, frankynsence, mastyke, comyne, lyneseed, and anyse seed, of everye one a lyke, pouder of osmonde rootes, that is to saye of the brode ferne, the .iiii. parte of all; make a playster with sufficient oyle olyve and fresshe swynes grece, and sprede it on a lether, and let it continue (except a great necessity) two or three weekes; after that, applye an other lyke tylle ye see amendment. In this case it is verye good to make a poudre of the heares of an hare, and to temper it with suger or conserva roses, and gyve it to the chylde twyes every day.

If it be above the age of .vii. yere, ye maye make a singuler receyte in drinke to be taken everye daye twyse thus

A drynke for one that is brosten.

Take matfelon, daysieis, comferye, and osmondes, of every one a lyke, seeth them in the water of a smythes forge, to the thyrde parte, in a vessel covered on a softe fyer; then strayne it and gyve to drynke of it a good draughte at ones, mornynge and evenyng, addynge evermore in hys meates and drynkes the pouder of the heare of an hare beynge dryed.

Of fallynge of the fundamente.

Many tymes it happeneth that the gutte, called of the Latynes rectum intestinum, falleth out at the fundament and can not be gotten in agayne wythout peyne and labour; whyche dysease is a common thynge in chyldren, commyng oftentymes of a sodayne colde or a longe laxe, and may wel be cured by these subscribed medicines.

If the gutte hath ben longe out and be so swollen that it cannot be reposed, or by coldenes of the ayre be congeled, the best counsell is to let the chylde syt on a hote bathe, made of the decoction of mallowes, holihocke, lyneseed, and the rootes of lyllies, wherein ye shall bathe the foundamente wyth a softe cloute or a sponge, and whan the place is suppled, thruste it in agayne; whyche done, then make a pouder thus.

A pouder for fallynge of the foundament.

Take the poudre of an hartes horne brent, the cuppes of acornes dryed, rose leaves dryed, goates clawes brent, the rynde of a pomegranate, and of galles, of everye one a portion. Make them in pouder, and strowe it on the fundament. It shal be the better yf ye put a lytle on the gutte afore it be reposed in the place, and after it be setled, to put more of it upon the fundament; then bynde it in wyth hote lynnen clothes, and gyve the chylde quynces or a rosted warden to eate wyth cinamone and suger.

An other good pouder for the same.

Take galles, myrre, frankynsence, mastyke, and aloes, of every one a lytle; make them in a pouder and strowe it on the place.

A lytle tarre wyth gosegrece is also verye good in thys case.

An other good remedye.

Take the wolle frome betwen the legges or of the necke of shepe whych is full of sweate and fattie; then make a juyce of unsette leekes, and dippe the wolle in it, and laye it to the place as hotte as maye be suffered; and whan it waxeth colde, remove it and apply an other hote. Thys is a very good remedy for fallynge of the fundament.

If the chylde provoke many tymes to seege and can expell nothynge, that dysease is called of the Grekes tenesmos; for the whyche it shall be verye good to applye a playster made of gardeyne cressys and comyne, lyke quantitye; frye them in butter, and laye it on the bellye as hote as he maye suffre.

It is also commended to fume the nether partes wyth turpentyne and pitche, and to sytte longe upon a bourde of ceder or juniper as hote as maye be possible.

Chafynge of the skynne.

In the flanckes, armholes, and under the eares, it chaunceth oftentymes that the skyn fretteth, eyther by the childes own uryne, or for the defaulte of wasshing, or elles by wrappynge and kepynge too hote.

Therfore in the begynnynge, ye shall annoynt the places with fresshe capons grece, then yf it wylle not heale, make an oyntment and laye it on the place.

An oyntement for chafyng and gallynge.

Take the roote of the floure deluyce dryed, of redde roses dryed, galingale and mastyke, of eche a lyke quantitye; beate them into moste subtyle pouder, then wyth oyle of roses, or of lyneseed, make a softe oyntment.

Item, the longes of a wether, dryed and made in very fyne pouder, healeth all chafynges of the skine. And in like maner the fragmentes of shomakers lether, brent and caste upon the place in as fyne pouder as is possyble, hath the same effecte, whych thyng is also good for the gallynge or chafynge of the fete of whatsoever cause it commeth.

Item, bean floure, barlye floure, and the floure of fytches, tempered wyth a lytle oyle of roses, maketh a soverayne oyntment for the same entent.

If the chafynges be great, it is good to make a bathe of holyhocke, dyl, violets and lineseed, with a lytle bran, then to washe the same places oftentymes, and laye upon the sore some of the same thynges.

The decoction of plantayne, bursa pastoris, horsetayle, and knotgrasse, is excedynge good to heale all chafynges of the skynne.

Of small pockes and measylles.

Thys dysease is common and familier, called of the Grekes by the generall name of exanthemata, and of Plinie papule et pituite eruptiones. Notwythstandyng, the consent of writers hath obteyned a destinction of it in .ii. kyndes, that is to saye: varioli the measels, and morbilli, called of us the small pockes.

They be bothe of one nature and procede of one cause, savynge that the mesyls are engendred of the inflammation of blood, and the smal pockes of the inflammation of bloode myngled wyth choler.

The sygnes of them bothe are so manifest to syght that they nede no farther declaration. For at the fyrste some have an ytche and a fretyng of the skyn, as yf it had ben rubbed wyth nettles, payne in the head and in the backe, the face redde in coloure and flecked, feare in the slepe, great thyrst, rednes of the eyes, beatynge in the temples, shotyng and pryckyng thorough all the bodye. Then anone after, when they breake out, they be sene of dyvers fasshyons and fourmes: somtyme as it were a drye scabbe or a leprye spreadyng over all the membres, other whyles in pushes, pimples, and wheles, rennyng with moch corruption and matter, and wyth greate peyne of the face and throte, dryenesse of the tonge, horcenes of voyce, and, in some, quiverynge of the harte wyth swownynge.

The causes of these evell affections are rehersed of authours to be chyefly foure:

Fyrste, of the superfluyties whyche myght be corrupte in the woumbe of the mother, the chylde there beyng and receyvynge the same into the poores; the whyche at that tyme for debility of nature coulde not be expelled but, the chyld increasynge afterwarde in strengthe, is dryven oute of the veynes into the upper skynne.

Secondarilie, it maye come of a corrupte generation, that is to saye whan it was engendred in an evyl season, the mother beynge sycke of her natural infirmitye. For suche as are begotten that tyme verye seldome escape the disease of leprye.

The thyrde cause maye be an evylle dyete of the nourse or of the chylde it selfe, whan they feade uppon meates that encrease rotten humours, as milk and fyshe both at one meale, lykewise excesse of eatynge and drynkynge and surfeyte.

Fourthlye, this dysease commeth by the waye of contagion whan a sycke person infecteth an other, and in that case it hath great affinitie wyth the pestylence.

Remedye.

The best and most sure helpe in this case is not to meddle wyth any kynde of medicines, but to let nature woorke her operation. Notwythstandynge, yf they be too slowe in commynge oute it shall be good for you to gyve the chyld to drinke sodden mylke and saffron, and so kepe hym close and warme whereby they maye the soner issue forthe, but in no case to administre anye thynge that might eyther represse the swellynge of the skynne or to coole the heate that is wythin the membres. For yf thys dysease, which shuld be expelled by a natural action of the body to the long healthe afterwarde of the pacient, were by force of medicine cowched in agayne, it were even ynough to destroye the chyld. Therfore, abide the ful breaking out of the sayd wheales, and then (yf they be not ripe) ease the chyldes peyne by makynge a bath of holihock, dil, camomyl, and fenel; yf they be rype and matter, then take fenell, wormewood, and sage, and seeth them in water to the thyrde part, wherin ye maye bathe hym with a fyne cloth or a sponge. Always provyded that he take no colde durynge the tyme of hys sycknesse.

The wyne wherin fygges have ben sodde is singuler good in the same case, and may be well used in all tymes and causes.

Yf the wheles be outragyous and great, with moche corrosion and venim, some make a decoction of roses and plantayne in the water of oke, and dissolve in it a lytle Englysh honye and camphore.

The decoction of water betonye is approved good in the sayde dyseases. Lykewyse the oyntment of herbes, wherof I made mention in the cure of scabbes, is excedynge holsome after the sores are rype.

Moreover it is good to droppe in the pacientes eyes, .v. or vi. tymes a daye, a lytle rose or fenel water to comforte the syght, lest it be hurte by contynuall renning of matter. This water must be mynistred in the somer colde, and in the winter ye ought to aply it luke warme.

The same rose water is also good to gargle in hys mouthe, yf the chylde be then payned in the throte.

And lest the condytes of the nose shuld be stopped, it shall be very expedient to let hym smell often to a sponge wete in the juce of saverye, stronge vynegre, and a lytle rosewater

To take awaye the spottes and
scarres of the smal pockes
and measels.

The blood of a bulle or of an hare is moche commended of authours to be annoynted hote upon the scarres, and also the lycour that yssueth out of shepes clawes or gootes clawes, hette in the fyer. Item, the dryppyng of a cygnet or swanne layed upon the places oftentymes hote.

Fevers.

Yf the fever use to take the child with a great shakyng and afterwarde hote, whether it be cotidian or tertian, it shall be singuler good to gyve it in drynke the blacke seedes of peonye made in fyne pouder, searced and myngled with a lytle sugre. Also take plantayne, fetherfew, and verveyn, and bathe the chylde in it ones or twyse a daye, bynding to the pulces of the handes and feet a playstre of the same herbes stamped, and provoke the chylde to sweate afore the fytte commeth.

Some gyve counsell, in a hote fever, to applye a colde playstre to the breest, made in this wyse. Take the juyce of wormewood, plantayne, mallowes, and houseleeke, and tempre in them as moch barlye floure as shal be suffycient, and use it. Or thus, and more better, in a weake pacyent:

Take drye roses and poudre them; then tempre the poudre wyth the juyce of endyve or purcelane, rose water, and barlye floure, and make a playstre to the stomake.

Item, an oyntment for hys temples, armes, and legges, made of oyle of roses and populeon, of eche lyke moche.

A good medicine for the ague in chyldren.

Take plantayne with the roote, and wash it; then seeth it in fayre runnynge water to the thyrde parte, whereof ye shall gyve it a draughte (yf it be of age to drynke) with sufficient sugre, and laye the sodden herbes, as hoote as maye be suffred, to the pulses of the handes and feet. This must be done a litle afore the fytte; and afterward cover it with clothes.

The oyle of nettles, wherof I spake in the title of styfnesse of lymmes, is excedynge good to annoynt the membres in a colde shakynge ague.

Of swellynge of the coddes.[39]

To remove the swellyng of the coddes procedynge of ventositie, or of any other cause (excepte brustynge), whether it be wyth inflammation or without, here shal be rehersed manye good remedyes of whyche ye maye use accordyng to the qualitye and quantitye of the gryefe; alway provided that, in this disease, ye maye in no case applye any repercussyves; that is to saye, set no colde herbes to dryve the matter backe, for it would then returne agayne into the body, and the congelation of suche a sinowye membre woulde peradventure mortifye the whole. And

---

[39] i.e., scrotum.

above al ye maye set no playster to the stones wherin hymlocke entereth, for it wyll depryve them for ever of theyr growynge, and not only them but the brestes of wenches whan they be annoynted therewyth, by a certeyne qualitye, or rather an evyl property, beynge in it.

A goodly playster for swellyng of the stones.

Take a quarte of good ale worte, and set it on the fyre to sethe wyth the crommes of browne bread strongly levened and a handefull of comyne or more in pouder; make a playstre wyth all thys and sufficiente beane floure, and applye it to the gryefe as hote as may be suffered.

An other.

Take cowes donge and seethe it in mylke, then make a playster and laye it metelye hote upon the swellynge.

An other.

Take comyne, anyseseed, and fenugreke, of eche a like portion; seeth them in ale and stampe them, then tempre them with fresh maye butter or a lytle oyle olyve, and applye it to the sore.

An other.

Take camomyll, holyhocke, lynseed, and fenugreke; seethe them in water, and grynde all togyther, then make a playster wyth an handfull of beane floure, and use it.

An other in the begynnyng of the griefe.

Yf there be moche inflammation or heate in the coddes, ye maye make an oyntment of plantayne, the whyte and yolke of an egge, and a portion of oyle of roses; styrre them well aboute, and applye it to the grefe twyse or thryse a day.

When the payne is intollerable and the chylde of age or of stronge complexion, yf the premisses wyll not helpe ye shall make a playstre after this sorte: Take henbane leaves, an handfull and an halfe, mallowe leaves an handfull; seeth them well in cleare water; then stampe them and styrre them, and, with a lytle of the broth, beane floure, barly floure, oyle of roses and camomyll suffycient, make it up and set it on the swellyng luke warme. Henbane, as Avicenne sayth, is excedynge good to resolve the hardnesse of the stones by a secret qualitie. Notwithstandynge, yf it come of wynde it shal be better to use the sayde playsters that are made with comyne, for that is of a singuler operation in dissolvyng wynde, as affirmith Dioscorides wrytyng of the qualities of cumyne.

Of sacer ignis or chingles.

In Greke herisipelas, and of the Latines Sacer ignis, our Englysshe women call it the fyre of Saynt Anthonye, or chingles; it is an inflammation of membres with excedyng burnynge and rednesse, harde in the feelynge, and for the mooste parte crepeth above the skynne or but a lytle depe within the flesshe

It is a grevous payne and maye be lykened to the fyre in consumyng. Wherfore the remedyes that are good for burnyng are also very holsome here in this case And fyrste, the greene oyntment of herbes descrybed in the chapter of ytche is of good effect also in this cure; moreover the medicines that are here described

Take at the pothecaries of unguentum Galeni an ounce and an halfe, oyle of roses two ounces, unguenti populeon one ounce, the juce of plantayne and nightshade one ounce or more, the whytes of thre egges, beate them altogyther, and ye shal have a good oyntment for the same purpose.

An other.

Take earthwormes and stampe them in vynegre, then annoynt the grefe every two houres

Item, the donge of a swanne, or in lacke of it the donge of a gose, stamped with the whyte and yolke of an egge, is good.

Item, doves donge stamped in salet oyle or other is a singuler remedye for the same purpose.

Of burnyng and scaldyng.

For burnyng and scaldyng, whether it be with fier, water, oyle, lead, pytche, lyme, or any such infortune: Ye muste beware ye set no repercussive at the fyrst, that is to saye, no medicine of extreme colde, for that myght chaunce to dryve the fervent heate into the synowes and so stoppe the poores that it coulde not issue; whereof shulde happen moche inconnvenience in a great burning (but in a smal it coulde not be so daungerous); wherfore, the best is when ye see a membre eyther brent or scalded as is sayde afore.

Take a good quantitie of bryne which is made of water and salt, not to exceadynge eygre or stronge but of a meane sharpenessse, and with a clout or a sponge bathe the membre in it colde, or at the leest blood warme, thre or foure houres togyther, the longer the better. For it shall aswage moche of the peyne, open the pores, cause also the fyre to vapoure, and gyve a great comfort to the weake membre Then annoynt the place wyth one of these medicynes:

Take oyle of roses one part, swete creme two partes, honye halfe a parte, make an oyntment and use it.

Item, all the medicines descrybed in the last chapiter are of greate effecte in this case, lykewyse the grene oyntment made of water betonye

Item, a soverayne medicyne for burnynge and scaldynge and all unkynde heates is thus made: Take a dosen or more of harde rosted egges, and put the yolkes in a pot on the fyre by themselfe without lycour, styrre them and braye them with a stronge hande tyl there aryse as it were a froth or spume of oyle to the mouthe of the vessell, then presse the yolkes and reserve the lycour. This is called oyle of egges, a very precyous thyng in the forsayde cure.

Morover there is an oyntment made of shepes dong fryed in oyle or in swines grece, then put to it a lytle waxe and use it.

Also, take quycke lyme and wasshe it in verjuce .ix. or .x. tymes; then mingle it with oyle and kepe it for the same entent.

Item, the juce of the leaves of lillies .v. partes, and of vyneegre one part, honye a lytle, maketh an excellent medicine not onelye for thys entent but for all other kynde of hote and rennyng ulcers.

Note that whatsoever ye use in this case it must be laide unto blood warme. Also, for avoydyng of a scarre, kepe the sore alwaye moyst with medicyne.

Of kybes.

The kybes of the heeles are called in Latyn perniones; they procede of colde, and are healed with these subscrybed remedies.

A rape rooté[40] rosted with a litle freshe butter is good for the same gryefe.

---

[40] i e , turnip; *Brassica rapa*

Item, a dosen fygges, sodden and stamped wyth a lytle goose grece, is good.

Earthe wormes, sodden in oyle, hath the same effecte.

Item, the skynne of a mouse, clapped al hote upon the kybe wyth the heare outwarde; and it shulde not be removed durynge .iii. dayes.[41]

A playster for a kybed heele.

Take newe butter, oyle of roses, hennes grece, of eche an ounce; put the butter and the grece in a bygge rape roote or, in lacke of it, a great apple or onyon, and whan it is roste softe, braye it wyth the oyle and laye it playsterwyse upon the kybe.

An other.

Take the meate of apples and rapes rosted on the coles, of eche .iii. ounces, fresh butter .ii. ounces, duckes grese or swannes grece an ounce; stampe them all in a morter of leade, yf it maye be had, or els grynde them on a fayre marble and use it.

Of consumption or leanesse.

Whan a childe consumeth or waxeth leane wythoute anye cause apparaunt, there is a bathe commended of authours to wasshe the chylde manye tymes, and is made thus:

Take the head and feete of a wether, seeth them tyll the bones fall asunder; use to bathe the chylde in this licour, and after annoynte hym wyth thys oyntement folowynge.

Take butter wythoute salte, oyle of roses and of vyolettes, of eche .i. ounce, the fatte of rawe porke, halfe an ounce, waxe a quarteron of an ounce; make an oyntment wherwyth the chylde muste be rubbed every daye twyse. Thys, with good fedyng, shall encrease his strength by the grace of God.

---

[41] Still a popular remedy in the next century, as recommended by the Wife in Beaumont's comedy *The Knight of the Burning Pestle* (1607):

> Faith, and those chilblains are a foul trouble. Mistress Merrythought, when your youth comes home, let him rub all the soles of his feet and the heels and his ankles with a mouse skin (3. 187–90).

Of gogle eyes.

This impediment is never healed but in a very yonge chylde, even at the begynnynge whereunto there is appoynted no manner kynde of medicine but onelye an order of kepynge; that is to saye, to laye the chylde so in hys cradelle that he maye beholde directe agaynste the lyght, and not to turne hys eyes on eyther of both sydes If yet he begynne to gogle, then set the cradell after such a fourme that the lyght may be on the contrary syde: that is, on the same syde from whence he turneth hys eyes, so that for desyre of lyghte he maye dyrecte them to the same part, and so by custome brynge them to the due fashion. And in the nyght there ought to be a candell set in lykewyse, to cause hym to behold upon it and remove hys eyes from the evel custome. Also grene clothes, yelowe, or purple, are verye good in thys case to be set, as is sayde afore.[42] Furthermore, a coyfe or a byggen[43] stondyng out besydes hys eyes, to constrayne the syght to beholde direct forwarde.

Of lyce.

Somtymes not only chyldren but also other ages are annoyed with lyce They procede of a corrupte humour, and are engendred wythin the skynne, crepyng out alyve thorough the poores; whiche, yf they begynne to swarme in excedyng nombre, that dysease is called of the Grekes Phthiryasys,

---

[42] Phaer clearly had Roesslin's *The Byrth of Mankynde* in mind (and perhaps at his elbow) as he wrote this section Jonas's translation reads as follows

Of google eyes or lokynge a squynt
Yf the chylde have google eyes or that it loke a squynt, then fyrst set the cradel in such a place that the lyght maye come directelye and ryght in the chyldes face neyther in the one syde neyther in the other, neyther above the heade, leste it torne the syghte after the lyght Also marke on whiche syde that the eyes do gogle, and let the lyghte come unto it on the contrary syde so to retorne the syght And in the nyght season set a candell on the contrarye syde so that by this meane the goglynge of the eyes may be retorned to the ryghte place And farther it shall be good to hange clothes of divers and freshe coloures on the contrary syde and spetially of the coloure of lyght grene or yelowe for the chylde shall have pleasure to beholde these strange coloures, and in retornynge the eye syghte towarde suche thynges it shalbe occasion to rectifye the syght agayne (T2v-T3r)

[43] a child's cap

whereof Herode dyed as is wrytten in the Actes of Apostles.[44] And among the Romaynes, Scilla,[45] whych was a great tyraunt, and many other, have ben eaten of lyce to deathe, whyche thynge, whan it happeneth of the plage of God, it is paste remedye, but yf it procedeth of a naturall cause, ye maye well cure it by the meanes folowynge.

Fyrste, let the paciente abstayne from all kynde of corrupte meates or that brede fleume; and, amonge other, fygges and dates muste in thys case be utterly abhorred. Then make a lavatory to wash and scoure the bodie twyse a day thus: Take water of the sea, or els bryne, and stronge lye of asshes, of eche a lyke portion, wormewood a handful, seth them a whyle, and after wasshe the bodye with the same licour.

A goodlye medicine for to
kylle lyce

Take the groundes or dregges of oyle aloes, wormewood, and the galle of a bulle or of an oxe; make an oyntement, whyche is singuler good for the same pourpose

An other

Take musterde, and dissolve it in vinegre wyth a lytle salte peter, and annoynt the places where as the lyce are wonte to breede.

Item, an herbe at the pothecaries called stavesacre, brymstone, and vynegre, is excedyng good.

It is good to gyve the pacient often in hys drynke pouder of an hartes horne brente.

Stavisacre wyth oyle is a marveylouse holsome thynge in this case

---

[44] Acts 12 21-3. Tyndale's translation reads as follows

And upon a daye appoynted Herode arayed him in royall apparell, and set him in his seate, and made an oraycon unto them And the people gave a shoute, sayinge it is the voyce of a God and not of a man And immediatly the angell of the Lorde smote him, because he gave not God the honoure, and he was eatyn of wormes, and gave up the gooste

[45] i e , Sulla, Lucius Cornelius Sulla Felix (138-78 BC) According to Plutarch, in *Lives of the Noble Grecians and Romanes* (North's trans), Sulla composed his own epitaph "no man did ever passe him, neither in doing good to his frendes, nor in doing mischiefe to his enemies" (4 113)

An experte medicine to dryve
awaye lyse.

Take the groundes or dregges of oyle or, in lacke of it, fresh swines grece, a sufficient quantitie, wherin ye shal chafe an ounce of quycksylver tyl it be all sonken into the grece; then take pouder of stavisacre serced, and myngle all togyther; make a gyrdyll of a wollen liste[46] meete for the myddle of the pacient, and al to annoynte it over wyth the sayde medicine Then let hym were it contynually nexte his skynne, for it is a synguler remedye to chase awaye the vermyn. The onely odour of quyckesylver kylleth lyce.

These shal be suffycient to declare at this tyme in this litle treatise of the cure of chyldren which, if I maye knowe to be thankefully receyved, I wil by Gods grace supplye more hereafter. Neyther desyre I any lenger to lyve than I wil employe my studyes to the honoure of God and profyt of the weale publike

Thus endeth *The Booke of Childerne*, composed by Thomas Phayer,
studiouse in medicine, and hereafter begynneth
The Regimente of Lyfe translated by the
same Thomas out of Frenche
into Englysshe newely
perused, corrected
and enlarged.

---

[46] a strip of cloth.

TEXTUAL NOTES

Keyed to pagination, the textual notes will list first the reading of this text, followed by a colon, then the reading of the copy text. The copy text throughout (O) is the Huntington Library copy of *STC* 11967 *The Boke of Chyldren*, by Thomas Phaer, collating A2–G8v in Jehan Goeurot's octavo *The Regiment of Lyfe*, trans. Thomas Phaer (London, 1544) No other copy of this edition exists.

The second edition of the *Short Title Catalogue of English Books 1475–1640* records a copy in the Library of the Royal College of Physicians of London, but a letter dated 14 January 1997 from Geoffrey Davenport, Librarian of the Royal College of Physicians declares the attribution to be in error.[1].

The Huntington Library copy text (O) is printed in black letter. It has both catchwords and two different running titles: *A preface to the reader* and, variant-spelled, *The boke/booke of chyldren* The type size of the preface is larger than that of the text. The larger type reappears in the first line of the concluding paragraph, beginning "Thus endeth" (77).

All substantive press variants will be noted using the following abbreviations:

O1. *STC* 11969
O2. *STC* 11970
O3. *STC* 11971 (Copy text, Neale & Wallis edn.)
O4. *STC* 11972
O5. *STC* 11974
O6. *STC* 11975

---

[1] According to Davenport, "[W]e do not have the copy of STC 11967, that the 2nd edition of STC credits us with—a 1544 edition of Goeurot *The regiment of lyfe*, lacking a title-page. Perhaps the confusion arose because our copy of former STC 11968, now 11966.5, was tentatively catalogued in the 1950s as [London, E. Whytchurch, 1544?] That edition of course does not include Phaer's *The booke of children* "

Q: *STC* 11976
N&W: *The Boke of Chyldren*, ed. A.V. Neale and Hugh R.E. Wallis (Edinburgh: E. & S. Livingstone, 1955).

27. 9. others: other.
     23. condemne. condempne.
     28. buy: bye. O5: bie. Q: buie.
28. 13. damnable: dampnable.
29. 12. *Regyment of Lyfe*: regyment of lyfe.
31. 8. tryte. O3–O6: true.
     18. declaration: declation
     24. faulte: faute.
32. 7. Aristotle: Aristole.
33. 26 Parsneppe: Pasneppe   Q Parsneppe
35. 18. Stoppyng of the bellye. Line missing in N&W.
     24. fundament: O3, O4. skynne. O6, Q: skinne.
38. 5 chafyngdysshe: chafyndysshe.
39. 19 off: of.
     21. whole: hole.
     26. whole: hole.
41. 29 dystylle stylle.
     34 dronken O3, O5: dronken is exceding good.
43. 26. xxxvi. O2–O6: xxxvii. Q: 37.
44. 10. reder. Nowe: reder, nowe
45. 25 bread: breed.
     29–30 *The Regyment of Lyfe*: the regyment of lyfe.
46. 3. Manardus: Manardns.
47. 35 faulte: faute
50. 1–2. nesyng pouder: nesyngpouder.
     20. vertues animall be infebled· O3 provides "be"
51. 9. There: Ther.
     20. gommes: gonmmes.
52. 29. ulcers, sores, and woundes. O3: ulcers.
53. 6. syrynge O1, N&W: sprynge
     11. defaulte: defaute.
54. 28. compounded: compouned.
     34 tree: tre.
57. 16 solemne: solempne
     25. bread· breed.
59. 28. paste: past.

	29. [it]: O3 provides "it."
60.	16. afore reherced· aforereherced.
61.	25. whole. hole.
62.	19. whole. hole.
64.	14. iii. houres to iiii.: iiii. houres to iiii.
66.	30. hotte: whotte.
67.	6–7. defaulte: defaute.
	33 measels: meas ls.
70.	33 whole: hole.
76.	1. Actes of Apostles: actes of apostles.
77.	16. *The Booke of Childerne·* the booke of childerne.
	18. *The Regimente of Lyfe*: the regimente of lyfe.

GLOSSARY OF AUTHORS

ARISTOTLE (384–322 BC). Greek philosopher and empirical scientific observer who developed a vast system of analysis covering logic, science, ethics, politics, rhetoric, and metaphysics. A student of Plato, he rejected Plato's mystical Theory of Forms to argue that form and matter are the inseparable constituents of all existing things.

ARNOLDE DE VILLA NOVA (c.1235–1311). Spanish physician and anatomist. A leading medical figure at the University of Montpellier in the last decade of the thirteenth century

AVICENNA (980–1037). Phaer's "Kyng Avicenne of Arabie" (28) was an Islamic philosopher and physician at the courts of Arabian nobility. His *Canon of Medicine* combined Roman and Arabic medical knowledge, and remained the standard medical text of Europe until the mid-seventeenth century.

AULUS GELLIUS (c.128–c 180) Roman author and grammarian. His widely-informed *Noctes Atticae* ranges across such diverse topics as law, grammar, religion, philosophy, and science.

CAMPEGIUS. Symphorien Champier (c.1472–1539). French physician, humanist, historian, and Neoplatonic author. He was founder of the Royal College at Lyons and an early European biographer of Avicenna.

CELIUS. Most likely Caelius Aurelianus, a Latin physician of the fifth century who translated Soranus's early work on gynecology.

CELSUS (c.50 BC–c.10 AD). Learned Roman encyclopedist, perhaps a physician, whose lengthy and complex work *De Medicina* covered a vast range of topics, including medical history, preservation of health, characteristics of inflammation, and the integration of physic and surgery.

DIOSCORIDES. Most likely a Greek military physician of the first century AD, he wrote the first systematic *Materia Medica*, including books on spices, salves, oils, plants, and animal products. His work became the basis for all future studies in European pharmacology and herbal medicaments.

FUCHSIUS. Leonhard Fuchs (1501-1566). German botanist and professor of medicine at Tübingen. His *De Historia Stirpium* was an influential work on botany, renowned for its artistic merit and accuracy of detail. The genus *Fuchsia* takes its name from him.

GALEN (129-199). Greek physician and anatomist from Pergamum in Asia Minor who became court physician in Rome. His voluminous medical writings, preserved in Latin translations of Arabic texts, were widely influential and authoritative in Renaissance Europe.

HORACE (65-8 BC). Roman poet, famous for his *Satires* and didactic work, the *Art of Poetry (Ars Poetica)*.

LEONELLUS. Lionello de Vittori (1450-1520). Italian physician and professor of medicine at the University of Bologna.

MANARDUS. Giovanni Manardi (1462-1536). Physician and professor at the University of Ferrara. The 1536 edition of his *Epistolae Medicinales* included a preface by Rabelais.

MARSILIUS FICINUS. Marsilio Ficino (1433-1499). Widely influential Italian humanist, Neoplatonic intellectual, and physician who, according to Phaer, "all men assente to be singularly learned" (28).

MUSA. Antonius Musa. Roman physician of the first century BC who numbered Augustus, Virgil, and Horace among his patients. Neale and Wallis note that his *De Herba Betonica* had been printed at Basel in 1528, perhaps accounting for Phaer's inclusion of him among "the men of hyghe learnynge nowe of oure dayes" (29). But Phaer may have in mind Antonio Musa Brasavola (1500-1555), a published herbalist and colleague of Manardus at Ferrara who, according to Nutton in "Rise of Medical Humanism," certainly exerted influence in Phaer's day.

OTHO BRUNFELSIUS. Otto Brunfels (1464–1534). German monk, herbalist, and physician, instructor at the surgical school of Strassburg and popularizer of humanistic medicine. His writings include *Herbarum Vivae Eicones* and *Weiber un Kinder Apothek*

PAULUS AEGINETA. Paul of Aegina. Alexandrian Greek physician of the seventh century AD and author of the widely influential *Epitome of Medicine* based primarily on Galen

PHAVORINUS. Favorinus of Arles (c 85–c.150) Greek philosopher and scholastic, born at Arles in present-day France He travelled widely and taught at various locations in Italy, Greece, and Asia.

PLATO (429–347 BC) Greek philosopher and founder of the Academy in Athens. His idealist thought, presented through the *Dialogues* of Socrates, profoundly influenced Christian theology and Western philosophy in general.

PLINIUS, PLINIE (24–79). Roman statesman and scholar known as Pliny the Elder (Gaius Plinius Secundus), he wrote a massive *Natural History* in thirty-seven books. He died of suffocation while observing the eruption of Mt. Vesuvius.

RASIS Rhases (c.850–925). Persian physician and author of many books and treatises, especially the work known in Europe as the *Almansor* Styled by Phaer as "a solemne practicioner among phisicions" (57), Rhases was renowned for his empirical sense, spirit of generosity, and wide learning.

RUELLIUS. Jean Ruel (1474–1537). French physician and professor at the University of Paris.

SEBASTIAN OF AUSTRIKE. One of Phaer's "men of hyghe learnynge nowe of oure dayes" (29), he reportedly lived in Alsace and wrote a commentary on the work of Paul of Aegina.

SERENUS: Quintus Serenus Sammonicus (d. 212). Learned Roman physician, said to have been murdered at a banquet to which he had been invited by the emperor Caracalla. His *De Medicina Praeceptis* is a lengthy didactic poem on popular remedies and magical formulae.

THEOPHRASTUS (370–288 BC). Greek philosopher and student of Aristotle, whose scientific researches he continued. The author of two botanical treatises, he is best known for his *Characters*, a collection of sketches of psychological types.

VIGO. Giovanni da Vigo (1460–1525). Italian surgeon, author of *Practica Copiosa in arte Chirurgia* (1514). Although superseded by the work of Ambroise Paré, Vigo was first to describe gunshot wounds and their treatments.

VIRGILL, VIRGIL (70–19 BC). Roman poet. Author of the *Eclogues*, the *Georgics*, and most especially the *Aeneid*, which exerted an immense influence on later classical and Renaissance literature. Phaer himself refers to Virgil as "that devyne Poet" (32), and was the first Englishman to attempt a translation of all twelve books of Virgil's *Aeneid*.

WILHEL PLACENTINO. William of Saliceto (c.1210–c.1280). Italian physician and surgeon who advocated a dynamic combination of both faculties in his seminal work *Chyrurgia*.

XENOPHON (c.428–c.354 BC). Greek historian and philosopher whose historical works include the *Anabasis* and the *Memorabilia*, as well as treatises on other subjects including politics, war, and horsemanship.

GLOSSARY OF MEDICINAL HERBS AND PLANTS

ALEHOFE *Nepeta*. A species of catnip.

ALOES *Aloe vera*. A well known skin-healing gel, also a bitter purgative.

AMEOS DORONISI. (Bishop's weed) *Aegopodium*. A glaucous annual native to the Mediterranean.

ANTINOMIE. (monkshood, wolfsbane) *Aconitum* Many important drugs are obtained from this species which can contain strong poisonous alkaloids.

ANYS or ANISE. A popular fragrant herb native to Egypt and the Mediterranean. Often used as a digestive aid, it was prescribed by Hippocrates for coughs.

BAYE. *Laurus nobilis*. This popular culinary herb is the classical symbol for greatness and reward. It reputedly soothes the stomach, relieves flatulence, and acts as a healing agent for rheumatism.

BEAR'S BREECH *Acanthus* Herbaceous perennial; classical decoration of Corinthian columns

BEETE. *Beta vulgaris*. Wild beet; ancestor of cultivated edible beets.

BETONY. *Stachys officinalis*. Tall European perennial widely popular as a medicinal herb and even accorded magical properties.

BLACKE BURIES. *Rubus fruticosus*. A widely naturalized berry plant native to Great Britain.

BURSA PASTORIS. Shepherd's purse.

CAMOMYLLE. *Chamaemelum nobile.* A popular "strewing" herb in medieval England used to freshen air in enclosed rooms. Useful internal antispasmodic and external anti-inflammatory, camomile was recommended by Dioscorides and Pliny for relief of headaches and for disorders of the kidneys, liver, and bladder.

CARRETTE or CARROT. *Daucus carota,* the popular root vegetable.

CASTOR. *Ricinus communis.* Now chiefly a laxative, castor oil was used in medieval Europe as a kind of liniment or lubricant. It contains a blood-coagulating protein (*ricin*) which makes unprocessed castor beans highly poisonous.

CELIDONYE. Greater Celandine. *Chelidonium majus.* Of the poppy family, this plant contains several alkaloids and has been used as a purgative, diuretic, diaphoretic, and expectorant. It has been popularly believed to cure warts.

CENTAURYE. Of the genus *Centaurea,* this plant is sometimes referred to by Phaer as Matfelon.

CHERITRE. Of the genus *Prunus;* refers to flowering deciduous trees.

CHESBOLLE. *Papaver somniferum.* Opium poppy.

CICORY or CHICORY. *Cichorium intybus.* A mild tonic and diuretic.

CLIMENO. *Convolvulus.* A genus of the morning glory family; a purgative described by Dioscorides in his *Herbal.*

CLOVES. *Syzygium aromaticum.* Dried flower buds of tropical evergreen, popular for aromatic, flavoring, and mildly anesthetic properties.

COLOCINTH. *Citrullus colocynthus.* Also known as bitter-cucumber, this gourd of India has purgative medicinal qualities. It may be the wild ancestor of the cultivated watermelon.

COMFERY or COMFREY. *Symphytum officinale.* Named from the

Latin *conferta*, to grow together, this herbaceous perennial reveals dense jointure of leaf base and stem upon which leaf is grown. According to the medieval "Doctrine of Signatures," such propensity indicates value for healing broken bones, sprains, and bruises.

CORALLINE. *Corallina officinalis* A seaweed.

CORTICUM THURIS. Aromatic bark of the desert evergreen Boswellia, also known as the "Frankincense tree."

CRESSIS. *Lepidium sativum*, common garden cress.

CUCUMBER. *Cucumis sativus*, common cultivated cucumber.

CUMMYN or CUMIN. Balsamic and highly flavored seeds of the cumin plant (*Cuminum cyminum*)

CYNAMOME or CINNAMON Bark of the cinnamon tree (*Cinnamomum zeylanicum*); a pungent, highy flavored astringent, stimulant, and carminative

DAYSE or DAISY. *Bellis perennis*, the common old-world "day's eye."

DOCK. Species of *Rumex*, high in vitamin C; used to treat scrofula and skin problems.

DRAGAGANT or TRAGACANTH. Medicinal gum of the shrub *Astragalus gummifer*.

DYLLE or DILL. *Anethum graveolens* A pickling spice, once popular medicinally as a carminative; also reputed to relieve babies with colic and to increase mother's milk.

ELDER. An ancient and powerfully medicinal plant of the genus *Sambucus*; the roots, stems, and leaves contain strong cyanogenic glucosides that release cyanide.

ENDIVE. *Cichorium endiva*. Lettuce-like vegetable plant native to India.

ERINGIUM. Root of the sea holly (*Eryngium maritimum*); once popular as an aphrodisiac.

EUPHORBIUM. Gum of the widely diverse Spurge family *Euphorbiaceae*.

FENELLE. *Foeniculum vulgare*. A carminative, mild diuretic, and stimulant, fennel is native to the Mediterranean and widely naturalized elsewhere for its culinary importance.

FENUGREKE. *Trigonella Foenum-graecum*. Widely popular folk cure-all, this annual herb of ancient Egypt was introduced to Europe in the ninth century by Benedictine monks.

FETHERFEW or FEVERFEW. *Chrysanthemum pathenium*. An anti-inflammatory, this herb has been well-documented in connection with relief of fever and aid in childbirth.

FITCHES or VETCHES. Herbaceous perennials of the species *Vicia*.

FLEWORT. A popular name for the genus *Erigeron* taking in many species belonging to the daisy family.

FLOURDELUYCE or FLEUR-DE-LIS. Of the genus *Iris*, adopted by Louis VII of France in 1147 as his personal emblem and the heraldic emblem of France. Popular medicinally since ancient times as a mild sedative.

FRANKENSENCE. Aromatic gum of the desert evergreen genus *Boswellia*.

FUMYTORY. Of the genus *Fumaria*, esteemed by ancient herbalists as a purifier of the blood and other disorders.

GALEOPSIS. The common English hemp nettle or bastard nettle *Galeopsis tetrahita*.

GALINGALE. Aromatic root of East Indian plants of the genera *Alpinia* and *Kaempferia*, much used in the medicine and cookery of Renaissance Europe.

GINGER. Root of the tropical perennial *Zingiber officinale*. A mild stimulant used to soothe indigestion.

GOURDE. Fruit of the widely-cultivated white-flowered gourd (*Lagenaria vulgaris*), best known for its decorative and domestic uses.

GROUNSWELL or GROUNDSEL. Of the popular and widely-distributed genus *Senecio*.

GUAIACUM. Resin of the Lignum-Vitae (*Guaiacum officinale*), a New World tree, distilled for use as an expectorant; once considered effective against gout and syphilis.

GUM ARABIKE. Gum collected from the tropical Acacia tree (*Acacia nilotica tomentosa*).

HEARTSEASE. *Viola tricolor*. The pansy known as Johnny-jump-up, native of Europe but widely naturalized in North America.

HENBANE. *Hyoscyamus niger*. Poisonous member of the nightshade family, famed for its medicinal and narcotic effects.

HOLY HOCKE or HOLLYHOCK. Popular garden perennial *Althaea rosea*.

HOOREHOUND. *Marrubium vulgare*. Ancient curative widely used as an expectorant.

HORSETAILE. *Equisetum*. Contains saponin and glycosides, accounting for mild diuretic action.

HOUSELEKE. *Sempervivum tectorum*. Also called Hen-and-chickens; used as a poultice on burns.

HUMLOCK or HEMLOCK. *Conium maculatum*. Poisonous, nonwoody member of the carrot family.

HYSOPE or HYSSOP. *Hyssopus officinalis*. Aromatic perennial used as a mild expectorant.

JEWES EAR. Edible fungus *Exidia auricula-judae* which grows on the elder tree.

IPERICON. St-John's-Wort of the family *Hypericaceae*. Widely distributed shrub and subshrub of temperate areas of the northern hemisphere. See also Tutsone.

KNOTGRASSE. Of the genus *Polygonum*; widely distributed herbaceous plants with swollen-jointed stems.

LECKE or LEEK. *Allium porrum*. Milder-flavored relative of the onion.

LETTUSE. *Lactuca sativa*. Widely popular salad vegetable.

LIGNUM ALOES. Wood of the resinous American bursera trees.

LIGNUM VITAE. Literally "wood of life"; the guaiacum tree.

LIND. Linden or lime tree of the genus *Tilia*.

LIQUIRICE or LICORICE. Taproot of the hardy perennial *Glycyrrhiza glabra*; medicinally varied, including use as a diuretic, demulcent, expectorant, mild laxative, and antispasmodic.

LYNESEDE. Seed of the common flax *Linum usitatissimum*.

MACES. Product of the nutmeg *Myristica fragrans*; specifically, a spice made from the outer coverings of nutmeg seeds.

MAJORAM or MARJORAM. *Origanum vulgare*. Widely popular folk medicine containing mild antioxidant and antifungal properties.

MALLOWES. *Malva sylvestris*. Tall annual, native to temperate and warm temperate parts of Europe and naturalized in North America.

MASTIKE. Gum of the Mediterranean mastic tree *Pistacia lentiscus*.

MATFELON. See Centaurye.

MEDLAR. Fruit of the medlar tree *Mespilus germanica*, common in Europe and southern England.

MELLILOTE. Tall sweet clover *Melilotus officinalis*.

MISTLETOW or MISTLETOE. Semiparasitic clumping shrub (*Viscum album*) of Europe containing toxic proteins.

MOREL. Common or black nightshade *Solanum nigrum*. Contains sedative proerties.

MUSCLE. See Mistletow.

MYNTE Of the genus *Mentha* popular as a flavorful carminative and gastric stimulant.

MYRRE. Resinous gum of the African shrub *Commiphora myrrha*.

NENUPHAR Water lily of the genus *Nymphaea*

NEPTE or NEPETA. *Nepeta cataria*. A species of catnip.

NETTEL. Common stinging nettle (*Urtica dioica*) of Europe.

NUTMIGGES or NUTMEG. Seed of the *Myristica fragrans*

ORGANYE Wild marjoram, *Origanum vulgare*. A mild tonic and stimulant.

OSMUNDE. European royal fern (*Osmunda regalis*).

PARIETARIE OF THE WAL. *Parietaria officinalis*. A nonstinging relative of the nettle renowned by Dioscorides for curing "all manner of inflammation."

PARSNEPPE or PARSNIP. *Pastinaca sativa*.

PELLITORY OF SPAYNE. *Anacyclus pyrethrum*. A prostrate perennial of the daisy family native to southeast Europe.

PEONIE. *Paeonia officinalis* Cultivated herbaceous flowering plant named for Paion, physician of the gods. Highly regarded in ancient medicine.

PHILIPENDULA. Dropwort. *Filipendula vulgaris*. Hardy herbaceous perennials of the northern hemisphere, their roots bear tuberous buds that suggest water or urine drops Hence its ascribed virtue in releasing urinary strictures.

PLANTAYNE. *Plantago major*. A sacred herb of the ancient Saxons; now a widely-established, even exasperatingly hardy, sub-shrub throughout temperate regions. Useful as a mild anti-inflammatory.

POMEGRANARD or POMEGRANATE. Fruit of the deciduous *Punica granatum*, cultivated since antiquity in the Middle East and in warm regions of the Mediterranean.

POPULEON. Balsamic ointment derived from poplar buds and containing anti-inflammatory and analgesic agents.

PURCELANE. Edible weed *Portulaca oleracea* cultivated since antiquity.

QUINCE Fruit of the quince tree *Cydonia oblonga*.

RADYSH or RADISH. Garden vegetable *Raphanus sativa*.

RAPE. Old World turnip, *Brassica rapa*

REWE or RUE. Folk antidote and charm, the "Herb of Grace" (*Ruta graveolens*) is more popular symbolically than medically.

ROCKET. *Eruca sativa*. Hot, highly-flavored salad plant of the Mediterranean region.

RYBWOORT. *Plantago lanceolata*. Of the plantain family.

SAFFRON *Crocus sativus* A popular culinary spice, saffron has traditionally been used against colds and as an appetite stimulant.

SAGE. *Salvia officinalis*. An aromatic culinary herb, sage contains volatile oils with antiseptic and astringent properties.

SAUNDERS. Aromatic sandalwood of the Indian evergreen *Santalum album*.

SAVEIN or SAVIN. *Juniperus sabina*. Native to central Europe and western Asia, the savin juniper contains poisonous oils used to induce abortion.

SAVERY or SAVORY. Summer (*Satureja hortensis*) or winter (*S montana*) variety—either is popular as a cooking spice. Summer savory contains mild antiseptic and astringent properties.

SCABIOUSE. Many varieties of *Scabiosa* inhabit Europe, Asia, and Africa. This hardy herbaceous perennial derives its name from the Latin *scabies* "itch," for which it was thought to be a cure.

SCOLITOBOTANI. See Coralline.

SMALLACH Wild celery (*Apium graveolens*), the foliage of which was probably poisonous

SORELL. *Rumex acetosa*. Cultivated species of dock, used for skin problems

SPIKE. Oil of *Lavendula spica* or English lavender, a popular aromatic and cleansing agent.

SPYKENARDE. Essential oil of the Asian herb *Nardostachys jatamansi*.

STAVESACRE Larkspur seeds (*Delphinium staphisagria*), containing poisonous properties.

TANSIE or TANSY. *Tanacetum vulgare*. A popular fragrant and medicinal plant of the ancients, tansy contains toxic substances

TUTSONE. St. John's wort. *Hypericum androsaemum*. A plant reputed to keep men and women chaste, according to medieval authorities.

TYME or THYME. *Thymus vulgaris*. Popular culinary herb and folk cure-all

VALERIAN. *Valeriana officinalis*. Containing carminative and antispasmodic properties, valerian is also popular for its tranquilizing effects.

VERVEYNE or VERVAIN. *Verbena officinalis*.

VIOLETTES Species of the genus *Viola*, especially sweet violet (*Viola odorata*). Once prescribed for disorders such as gout and spleen, the violet contains antiseptic and expectorant properties.

WALWORT *Sambucus ebulus*. See Elder.

WARDEN. An old European variety of pear.

WATER BETONY. Figwort. *Scrophularia aquatica*.

WATER PLANTAYNE. *Alisma plantago*.

WORMESEDE. *Erysimum cheiranthoides*. Once grown as a popular cure for worms in children.

WORMWOOD. *Artemisia absinthium*. Used since ancient times as a worming medicine, wormwood contains thujone, a convulsant poison and narcotic.

ZEDOARY. Aromatic root of of the East Indian curcurma plant; turmeric.

WORKS CITED

Anderson, Benedict. *Imagined Communities: Reflections on the Origin and Spread of Nationalism.* Rev. ed. London: Verso, 1991.
Arber, Agnes. *Herbals, Their Origin and Evolution: A Chapter in the History of Botany.* 2nd ed. Darien, CT. Hafner, 1970.
Ariès, Philippe. *Centuries of Childhood: A Social History of Family Life.* Trans Robert Baldick. New York: Vintage, 1962.
Beaumont, Francis. *The Knight of the Burning Pestle.* Ed. Michael Hattaway. New Mermaids. London: A. & C. Black, 1986.
Berry, Boyd M. "The First English Pediatricians and Tudor Attitudes Toward Children." *Journal of the History of Ideas* 35 (1974): 561-77.
Bindoff, S. T. *The House of Commons 1509-1558.* Vols 1, 3 London: Secker & Warburg, 1982.
Campbell, Lily B., ed. *The Mirror for Magistrates* 1938; repr. New York: Barnes & Noble, 1960.
Churchyard, Thomas. "Preface" to John Skelton, *Pithy, Pleasant, and Profitable Works.* 1568; repr. Menston, Yorkshire: Scolar Press, 1970.
Cule, John. "Thomas Phaer MD of Cilgerran (1510-60)." *Medical History* 30 (1986). 90-91.
Cunningham, Peter. "The Will of Thomas Phaer." *The Shakespeare Society's Papers* 4 (1849): 1-5.
deMause, Lloyd. "The Evolution of Childhood." *The History of Childhood,* ed. Lloyd deMause, 1-73. New York: Psychohistory Press, 1974.
Demers, Patricia. *Heaven Upon Earth: The Form of Moral and Religious Children's Literature, to 1850.* Knoxville: Univ. of Tennessee Press, 1993.
di Porcia, Jacopo *The Preceptes of Warre.* Trans. Peter Betham. STC 20116 London, 1544.
Donnison, Jean *Midwives and Medical Men: A History of the Struggle for the Control of Childbirth.* London: Historical Publications, 1988.
Eamon, William. *Science and the Secrets of Nature: Books of Secrets in Medieval and Early Modern Culture.* Princeton: Princeton Univ. Press, 1994.

Eccles, Audrey. "The Reading Public, the Medical Profession, and the Use of English for Medical Books in the 16th and 17th Centuries." *Neuphilologische Mitteilungen* 75 (1974): 143–56.

———. "The Early Use of English for Midwiferies 1500–1700." *Neuphilologische Mitteilungen* 78 (1977): 377–85.

———. *Obstetrics and Gynaecology in Tudor and Stuart England*. Kent: Kent State Univ. Press, 1982.

Eisenstein, Elizabeth L. *The Printing Press as an Agent of Change*. 2 vols. Cambridge: Cambridge Univ. Press, 1979.

Elyot, Sir Thomas. *The Castel of Helth*. London, 1541.

Fuller, Thomas. *History of the Worthies of England*. Wing F2440. London, 1662.

Furnivall, F. J., ed. *The Babees Book*. London: Early English Text Society, 1868.

Gellius, Aulus. *The Attic Nights of Aulus Gellius*. 3 vols. Trans. W. Beloe. London: J. Johnson, 1795.

Goeurot, Jehan. *The Regiment of Lyfe*. Trans. Thomas Phaer. STC 11967. London, 1544.

———. *The Regiment of Life*. The English Experience 802. Amsterdam: Theatrum Orbis Terrarum, 1976.

Googe, Barnabe. *Selected Poems of Barnabe Googe*. Ed. Alan Stephens. Denver: Alan Swallow, 1961.

Gottfried, Robert S. *Doctors and Medicine in Medieval England 1340–1530*. Princeton: Princeton Univ. Press, 1986.

Hall, Arthur. *Ten Books of Homers Iliades, translated out of the French*. STC 13630. London, 1581.

Hampton, Christopher. *The Ideology of the Text*. Milton Keynes: Open Univ. Press, 1990.

Hanawalt, Barbara A. *Growing Up in Medieval London: The Experience of Childhood in History*. New York: Oxford Univ. Press, 1993.

Hasler, P. W. *The House of Commons 1558–1603*. Vol. 3. London: H. M. Stationery Office, 1981.

Hornblower, Simon and Anthony Spawforth. *Oxford Classical Dictionary*. 3rd ed. Oxford: Oxford Univ. Press, 1996.

Jones, W. J. *The Elizabethan Court of Chancery*. Oxford: Clarendon Press, 1967.

Lally, Steven, ed. *The "Aeneid" of Thomas Phaer and Thomas Twyne*. New York: Garland, 1987.

Lee, Sidney. "Phaer, Thomas." *Dictionary of National Biography*, Vol. 15: 1026–27. London: Smith, Elder & Co., 1909.

Lupton, Deborah. *Medicine as Culture: Illness, Disease and the Body in Western Societies* London: Sage, 1994.

Marlowe, Christopher. *Dido Queen of Carthage.* Ed. H. J. Oliver. Revels Plays. Cambridge: Harvard Univ. Press, 1968

Nashe, Thomas. "Preface to *Menaphon*." *The Life and Complete Works in Prose and Verse of Robert Greene.* Vol 6. Ed. Alexander B. Grosart. New York: Russell and Russell, 1964.

Nutton, Vivian. "Humanist Surgery." *The Medical Renaissance of the Sixteenth Century,* ed. A. Wear et al., 75-99. Cambridge: Cambridge Univ. Press, 1985.

———. "The Rise of Medical Humanism. Ferrara, 1464-1555." *Renaissance Studies* 11 (1997). 2-19.

Phaer, Thomas (Trans.). *Natura Brevium, Newly Corrected in Englysshe* STC 18402.5. London, 1530?.

———. *A New Boke Of Presidentes.* STC 3327. London, 1543.

——— *The Boke of Chyldren.* STC 11967. London, 1544.

———. *The Boke of Chyldren.* Ed. A. V. Neale and Hugh R. E. Wallis. Edinburgh: E. & S. Livingstone, 1955.

——— Trans *The Seven First Bookes of the Eneidos of Virgill.* STC 24799 London, 1558

———. Trans. *The Nyne Fyrst Bookes of the Eneidos of Virgil.* STC 24800. London, 1562.

Plutarch. *The Lives of the Noble Grecians and Romanes.* 8 vols Trans. Sir Thomas North. Oxford: Basil Blackwell, 1928.

Pollock, Linda A. *Forgotten Children: Parent-Child Relations from 1500 to 1900* Cambridge: Cambridge Univ. Press, 1983.

Puttenham, George *The Arte of English Poesie.* Ed. Edward Arber. London: Constable and Co., 1906.

Radbill, Samuel X. "Pediatrics." *Medicine in Seventeenth Century England,* ed Allen G. Debus, 237-82. Berkeley. Univ. of California Press, 1974.

Roberts, R. S "The Personnel and Practice of Medicine in Tudor and Stuart England. Part I: The Provinces." *Medical History* 6 (1962): 363-82.

Roesslin, Eucharius. *The Byrth of Mankynde.* Trans. Richard Jonas. STC 21153. London, 1540

Ruhräh, John *Pediatrics of the Past.* New York: Paul B. Hoeber Inc., 1925.

Siegel, Rudolph E. *Galen's System of Physiology and Medicine.* Basel. S. Karger, 1968.

Siraisi, Nancy G. *Medieval & Early Renaissance Medicine.* Chicago: Univ. of Chicago Press, 1990.
Slack, Paul. "Mirrors of Health and Treasures of Poor Men: The Uses of the Vernacular Medical Literature of Tudor England." *Health, Medicine and Mortality in the Sixteenth Century,* ed. Charles Webster, 237-73. Cambridge: Cambridge Univ. Press, 1979.
Smith, Michael B. H. and William Feldman. "Over-the-counter Cold Medications: A Critical Review of Clinical Trials Between 1950 and 1991." *Journal of the American Medical Association* 269 (May 5, 1993): 2258-63.
Still, George Frederic. *The History of Paediatrics.* 1931; repr. London: Dawsons, 1965.
Tittler, Robert. *Nicholas Bacon: The Making of a Tudor Statesman.* Athens: Ohio Univ. Press, 1976.
Towler, Jean, and Joan Bramall. *Midwives in History and Society.* London: Croom Helm, 1986.
Tucker, M. J. "The Child as Beginning and End: Fifteenth and Sixteenth Century English Childhood." *The History of Childhood,* ed. Lloyd deMause, 229-57. New York: Psychohistory Press, 1974.
Turner, William. *The Names of Herbes.* London, 1548.
———. *A New Herball.* Ed. George T. L. Chapman and Marilyn N. Tweddle. Cambridge: Cambridge Univ. Press, 1989.
Tyndale, William. Trans. *The New Testament (1534).* Ed. N. Hardy Wallis. Cambridge: Cambridge Univ. Press, 1938.
Vicary, Thomas. *The Anatomie of the Bodie of Man.* Ed. F. J. Furnivall. London: Early English Text Society, 1888.
Virgil. *Georgics. Virgil's Works.* Trans. J. W. Mackail. New York: Modern Library, 1934.
Voigts, Linda Ehrsam. "Editing Middle English Texts: Needs and Issues." *Editing Texts in the History of Science and Medicine,* ed. Trevor H. Levere, 39-68. New York: Garland, 1982.
———. "What's the Word? Bilingualism in Late-Medieval England." *Speculum* 71 (1996): 813-26.
Webbe, William. *A Discourse of English Poetrie.* STC 25172. London, 1586.
Wood, Anthony à. *Athenae Oxonienses.* Vol. 1. 1813; repr. New York: Johnson Reprint Corp, 1967.

Lightning Source UK Ltd.
Milton Keynes UK
UKHW020743270722
406450UK00005B/588